THE
WISDOM *to* KNOW
THE
DIFFERENCE

AN ACCEPTANCE & COMMITMENT THERAPY WORKBOOK *for* OVERCOMING SUBSTANCE ABUSE

KELLY G. WILSON, PhD
and TROY DuFRENE

NEW HARBINGER PUBLICATIONS, INC.

Distributed in Canada by Raincoast Books

Copyright © 2012 by Kelly G. Wilson and Troy DuFrene
New Harbinger Publications, Inc.
5674 Shattuck Avenue
Oakland, CA 94609
www.newharbinger.com

Cover design by Amy Shoup
Text design by Michele Waters-Kermes
Acquired by Catharine Meyers
Edited by Heather Garnos

Library of Congress Cataloging-in-Publication Data

Wilson, Kelly G.
  The wisdom to know the difference : an acceptance and commitment therapy workbook for overcoming substance abuse / Kelly G. Wilson, Troy DuFrene.
     p. cm.
  Includes bibliographical references.
  ISBN 978-1-57224-928-8 (pbk.) -- ISBN 978-1-57224-929-5 (pdf e-book)
  1. Change (Psychology) 2. Acceptance and commitment therapy. I. DuFrene, Troy, 1972- II. Title.
  BF637.C4W557 2012
  616.86'03--dc23

                        2011039770

19   18   17

15   14   13   12   11   10   9   8   7

CONTENTS

ACKNOWLEDGMENTS

It takes a whole lot of people to make a book like this, and there's little chance we'll remember them all. Much gratitude goes out to our mentors, teachers, students, confreres, comrades, and friends, all of whom materially contributed to the work.

Special thanks to folks at New Harbinger whose commitment to our work has been unflagging: Matt McKay, Catharine Meyers, Michele Waters, and all the rest. And to our peerless editor, Heather Garnos, whose literary deftness and wicked backhand quite literally beat the book into completion, much love and fathomless gratitude.

We gratefully acknowledge Mick Carnett's careful read, huge encouragement, exotic coffee contributions, and careful suggestions. Deep bow. Also to Maureen Flynn, who has worked very, very hard with me on some of the ideas found in this book.

Prologue

A PERSONAL STORY

God, grant me the serenity to accept the things I can't change,
the courage to change the things I can,
and the wisdom to know the difference.

You are not alone. I know the depths to which addiction can take a person, and I know something about recovery. I know it personally, and I know it as a scientist, therapist, and researcher. Woven into this book will be sensibilities science has to offer to the recovering person, but also some small bits and pieces of my own path in recovery and, finally, stories I've heard along the way.

The recovery process has been slow at times, even slower than baby steps. The best I've done some days was to sit on my hands. I've learned to appreciate even those days. If I'm sitting on my hands, it's very hard to make much mess to clean up later.

I started down this road something like twenty-five years ago. There was a time, in the winter of 1985, when I would be up in the night, lying on the bathroom floor, heartsick, alone, the house quiet all around me. Lying on that floor, between bouts of retching, I found myself in a dreadful spot—impossibly trapped between an absolute inability to drink anymore and an absolute inability to stop. Lying on that floor, I could feel the cool of the linoleum on my cheek and it was good. There in the bathroom, in the middle of the night, tortured, I found a moment's rest, my cheek pressed to the cool floor. My whole world was reduced to six square inches of cool linoleum. I could not leave that room without the terrors welling up around me. Even trying to rise from the floor filled me with awareness of all that I had done and regretted—and not done, and regretted more.

It was a starting point. From there, people began to teach me about acceptance and about holding my story in the world a little more gently, about letting go of limitations and opening up to possibility. By inches, I made my way up off the floor and out of that bathroom. I became engaged in the world in new ways. When I look where acceptance, openness, and engagement have taken me over the years, I have to pinch myself. I've fallen in love with people all over the world. I've become intimate with people and places and ideas that I could not have imagined. I've found souls all along the way who saw possibilities in me that I could not see in myself. And I've in turn had the privilege of seeing in others strength and beauty and possibility that they could not see in themselves.

And I can count a lot of days, a lot, between that barren winter of '85 and this day, this morning, this moment—a lot of days when the best I could do was sit on my hands. And, today, I count those days sitting on my hands as good days. All in a row they brought me right here together with you.

Rest a while. There will be time. Perhaps we can sit together on our hands today. And tomorrow, there won't be much mess to clean up. And we'll rise together and sweep up and go about our day as best we're able.

So if today is a day of hand-sitting, think of it as practice. The day will surely come when someone in need calls out. We're not likely to be able to reach out and reverse time in their world—bring parents back from the dead, retrieve a lost opportunity or a lost love—any more than we can turn back the clock in our own world. But perhaps if we have practiced, we can sit with them, on our hands if it's that kind of day, but together. And perhaps we'll find a way in this world, just as it is, to fall in love, and see beauty and strength and possibility together.

If you're reading this book, you know something about suffering. You know something about being stuck. Maybe you've sunk to the depths I had sunk to that dreadful winter of 1985. Perhaps farther, perhaps not so far. Still I will assume that you know something: something about despair, something about struggle, something about feeling trapped. You know that one's own personal hell is always the one that burns hottest.

So, I offer this little book as a way of extending my hand to you. Twenty-five years ago a fellow named Tom extended his hand to me in my darkest hour. At the time, I wondered what his angle was, what advantage he hoped to gain. I had nothing really to offer in return. I lost track of Tom and it took a few years to sort out what he had wanted from me. Here is what he wanted: if that hand up helped me to find my feet in this world and helped to set me on a path, if that hand up moved my life to an inexplicably and unexpectedly better place, someone would eventually reach out to me for help. Tom knew that. When that day came, life would ask me a question: will you reach back? Tom's hand was offered to me twenty-five-odd years ago in a locked psychiatric hospital in Seattle. It's in the spirit of the kindness of that offered hand that I offer mine to you in the form of this book. Welcome. Welcome.

1

Many Paths to Recovery, but Only One for You

There are certainly many paths to recovery. But you'll only take one. What's the best choice for you? We don't know. And you can never really know. You only get to live life once. However you live it, you won't know how it would have gone had you lived it differently. Time runs in one direction. Scientific studies often tell us what happened *on average* to the people who got this or that treatment. We'll cite some statistics in this book. But at the end of the day you won't have something happen to you on average. Something very particular will happen to you. The best measure—and we'll emphasize this over and over again—is how your path to recovery is working in your own life. We'll hold onto this practical theme throughout.

What Lies Ahead

Our initial drafts of this book began without much in the way of introduction. Our intention was to not waste words talking about theories and principles. We wanted to get immediately to sharing things that would be of use to you as you move toward recovery. And in the end we remain committed to this approach. Kind friends, however, prevailed upon us during the writing process to offer a few words of introduction.

The substance of this book is grounded in a model of psychotherapy called *acceptance and commitment therapy* (ACT from here on, which should be pronounced as a word rather than separate letters.) ACT is an application of a discipline in psychology called *behavior analysis*. Unless you have an interest in the study of psychology, the only thing we want you to take away from this fact is that we're concerned here with your behavior, with what you do, far more than we are with what you think or who you "are" in some abstract sense. Rather than explain too much about how ACT works as a model of psychotherapy, we'd rather keep writing to you about the issue of addiction and recovery and let the details of the approach come out in the process, in a commonsense, storytelling way rather than a deliberately professional or scholarly-seeming way. We will offer that the principles of ACT are being evaluated on an ongoing basis in research facilities all over the world, and that, from its earliest days, ACT has been applied to substance-abuse issues with good results. While what follows isn't science, it is *of* science. This is important to us, and we hope it's of some reassurance to you.

BLENDING ACT AND 12-STEP

While this book is grounded in ACT, we've chosen to devote space in this book to discussing how an ACT approach to recovery can be woven into a 12-step recovery process, the kind of approach you would encounter at Alcoholics Anonymous (AA) or Narcotics Anonymous (NA). ACT and 12-step are not a perfect fit for each other, but we think that they touch at enough points to make the two approaches work together well. In fact, we think there is an opportunity for the two models to support and inform each other.

We deliberately use the words "support and inform" with some care. This isn't an AA book, and we are not proposing to speak authoritatively about AA or its methods. We believe, though, that AA's basic writings suggest no one is in a position to speak or write this way. We recognize wisdom in the AA steps and traditions, and we acknowledge that many, many people have found their way out of addiction and to richer, more meaningful lives with the help of AA. We also note that AA comes from a storytelling tradition, a tradition that is grounded in the stories of its members and in the insight of their collective experience, rather than from a tradition of empirical observation, of science. We base this book on our assumption that the science-based principles of ACT and the narrative-evolved principles of AA, even if not a perfect match for one another, do overlap and interact in interesting ways. We believe that ACT can blend with and support AA recovery and, at the same time, lend the AA tradition the rigor of the laboratory.

How will this work? In the chapters that follow, we'll break from time to time to relate the ACT material in the chapter to a touch point of the 12-step approach. We'll pull this material out of the normal flow of the text. If it interests you, read it. If not, feel free to disregard it. In an afterword to this book, we've included some thoughts on 12-step. If you're involved in 12-step or considering becoming involved, you can take a look. The majority of the book doesn't depend on the 12-step model or your participation in it.

We include this material in the book in the full knowledge that many people in both the AA and the behavior science communities might disagree with us about this compatibility. Our hope is that you, reader, will enjoy the freedom to decide whether this book is useful to you without the distraction of any discussions of ideology or what is "right."

By way of introduction, we are collectively Kelly Wilson and Troy DuFrene. Kelly is a professor of psychology at the University of Mississippi in Oxford, Mississippi. He was one of three authors of the book *Acceptance and Commitment Therapy*, the book that laid the foundation for the evolving ACT research, study, and treatment communities. Kelly has been actively involved in substance-abuse treatment for more than twenty years and has personal experience with addiction and recovery. When the narrative of this book is expressed in the first person singular, you are reading Kelly's voice alone. Troy is a writer who happened, in one of those strange ways things sometimes turn out, to stumble into the ACT research community in 2006. Moved by the ideas he discovered there, he lingered and teamed up with Kelly to write *Mindfulness for Two* (2008) and *Things Might Go Terribly, Horribly Wrong* (2010).

We offer this book to you in service, fellowship, and friendship. Our sincere hope is that the book is of service to you—that it helps you get where you want to go.

To Abstain or Not to Abstain

Some people claim that there's a single inevitable course for untreated substance dependence: an inevitable downward spiral. Research studies don't support this claim (Vaillant 1995). Some people drink or use heavily and then stop and don't use at all. Some drink and use heavily and then go back to nonharmful patterns of use. Some drink and use heavily and then go through periods of nonharmful use followed by periods of harmful drug and alcohol use. We won't mince words: we firmly believe that the decision whether to abstain is yours and yours alone. Our purpose in this book isn't to convince you to quit. There's nothing in ACT that says that people should abstain entirely from addictive substances. What we've written here we offer as help and support for the decisions you have made or may make with regard to your own recovery. (We also acknowledge here that abstinence is at least popularly linked to 12-step recovery approaches such as Alcoholics Anonymous. We have more to say about this in the afterword to this book, Some Thoughts on the 12-Step Approach.)

Reasons to Abstain

That said, we're not telling you not to quit, either. The decision about whether to abstain or control your use of alcohol or drugs, while ultimately personal, is not one to be taken lightly. If you haven't given significant time to that question, we recommend you do so now. As you think it over, we recommend careful consideration of the alternatives.

The outcome you want from addiction treatment is centrally important to the treatment itself. Without a doubt, some people succeed, through treatment, at moderating their drinking. But there are undeniable risks that come with an attempt at moderation. If you're considering moderation as an approach to dealing with your substance abuse problem, we'd ask you to consider what would have to happen for you to pronounce your efforts a failure. And by consider we mean *seriously* consider. Below are a few things to think about that weigh on the side of abstinence.

You won't die from quitting. One consideration is that no one ever died from letting go of addictive substances. Some things with which people have problems, like eating, are necessary. You've got to eat. But many of these things are not necessary for survival. It's simply not a biological imperative that you drink or use drugs. You needn't ride a motorcycle at excessive speeds without a helmet, gamble beyond your means, or engage in daily anonymous sexual encounters, yet all of these carry significant personal risks. And if you feel compelled to engage in these activities when doing so comes at the expense of other areas of your life that matter to you, we would argue that the prospect of not engaging in these activities deserves very long and careful consideration. We're absolutely not going to tell you to quit. The choice to engage in any and all activities—including drinking or using drugs—in your life is absolutely yours and yours alone. (And, yes, we realize that this absolute freedom is scary and can, itself, be a source of considerable anxiety for you. We'll have more to say about that later.)

Habitual behavior is hard to control, especially when you're on autopilot. A lot of our behaviors are sort of automatic. Perhaps you've noticed this in your own life in areas outside addiction. For example, Kelly was always taught to clean his plate at dinnertime. He grew up working class, and wasting food was a serious no-no. It has been a huge effort for him, as an adult, to decide when to quit eating based on how his stomach feels rather than by whether his plate is empty or not. He's gradually learning that he doesn't have to fill his plate. And, even if he does fill it, he doesn't have to empty it. And he doesn't typically go to buffets. Why? Although he no longer piles his plate high, he also seldom, very seldom, eats a minimal portion when he goes to a buffet. Some circumstances make some behaviors more likely (and, often, make them happen automatically). If you're having problems with addiction, you don't want to be spending time on autopilot, especially when addictive substances are involved.

Some substances make it easier to use other substances or more of the same substance. Some substances—and alcohol is a great example—lower your inhibitions when you use them. You know when you want to do something and that little voice in the back of your head tells you not to for some reason? Some substances incline you to pay less attention to that little voice. So, for example, if you're at the bar and the band starts playing, you might be a little reluctant to step out on the dance floor. You want to, but you feel a little inhibited. If you have a couple of drinks, the inhibition melts away. This isn't in and of itself a bad thing, particularly if what you feel inhibited about is asking someone to dance. But what if the thing you feel like doing but feel inhibited about is having another drink or using some cocaine? Alcohol has the same effect on those inhibitions. In AA, they sometimes say, "One drink. One drunk." This isn't strictly true, but there's some basis for concern. Being able to accurately estimate one's blood alcohol does not make a person immune from decreased inhibition or lapses in judgment. There are good reasons that there are laws against driving while under the influence of even a small amount of alcohol. A lack of inhibition and poor judgment when you're piloting a ton of steel at high speed toward trees and cliff edges and other people can have disastrous consequences.

One of the most favorable circumstances for using substances is using substances. This probably sounds like word play, but it's not. When you go to the supermarket, they have people in the aisles to give you little bites of food. If you eat a little, it sometimes cues eating a lot. Free samples are not really free. Like an old potato chip commercial used to say, "Bet you can't eat just one." This isn't necessarily anything specific to addictive substances; it's also true of a lot of other things in our lives. The difference is that those other things have likely not caused you the same level of problems as drugs and alcohol. You've probably never lost a job from eating too many potato chips or crashed your car after too much chocolate or had your spouse file for divorce after buying a gallon-size jar of artichoke hearts. And we're not suggesting that one chip inevitably leads to another. It simply increases the chances that you'll keep indulging until the bag is empty (or you run out of dip.) Likewise, taking one drink increases your odds for taking another, and this will ever be the case. Given this truism, it's well worth your time to consider very, very carefully if you want to put yourself in that position. You must ask yourself, *Is the increase in likelihood worth it to me at this point in my life?*

Moderate drinkers often don't stay moderate for long. While we don't know of any strong evidence that suggest that drinking always leads to more drinking, there's considerable evidence that drinking predicts drinking and that more drinking predicts more drinking. Although the use of a little bit of a substance may or may not send you into a spiral of intoxication, it certainly increases the risk of more use. For example, in a very large clinical trial for alcoholism treatment called Project Match, patients were divided into three groups based on their drinking patterns during the year following treatment: one group abstained, a second drank moderately, and a third group drank heavily. If we look at the number of people in the abstaining, moderate, and heavy drinking groups, we find that at year three, the majority of the abstainers (71 percent) were still abstainers. The majority of the heavy drinkers (78 percent) were still heavy drinkers. The majority of the moderate drinkers, however, were no longer classifiable as moderate drinkers. Twenty-seven percent had become abstainers and 50 percent relapsed to heavy drinking (Maisto et al. 2006).

These data suggest a few things. First, they suggest that some individuals, though diagnosed with alcohol dependence, do moderate their drinking and continue to stay moderate over time. However, many don't. Another thing suggested by these data is that a substantial number of individuals may ultimately find their way to abstinence, for whatever reason, even though they don't start out planning to abstain.

Reasons to Keep Drinking and Using

Different drugs, and alcohol especially, are a big part of our culture. Depending on your social network, many events in your life may have drinking or drug use as a social component. If you make the decision to abstain, it's likely, especially in the initial stages of recovery, that you'll feel awkward in these settings. Many people will have opinions on whether you should drink or use. Some will actively offer you something to drink, a toke, or a line. A few will actively attempt to undermine your resolve. Social discomfort isn't insignificant.

Kelly has had some personal experience in this regard that you may find interesting. As a psychologist, academic, and scientist, he goes to many conferences every year. The cocktail lounges at big convention hotels are a sort of social magnet. A lot of papers, research projects, and collaborations have been started in those lounges. Kelly has reported to his station in cocktail lounges all over the world for more than twenty-five years. He loves hanging out and talking shop.

From time to time in these situations, a newer colleague will offer to buy him a drink. He politely refuses. The colleague insists. Kelly refuses again. The colleague persists: just a sip. Kelly tells the colleague that he doesn't drink alcohol. Kelly has had a number of individuals over the years ask him when he stopped drinking. Without exception, Kelly stopped drinking long before he ever met the individual asking the question. Some have refused to believe it. He's had people who have sat in cocktail lounges with him for more than a decade who never noticed that he wasn't drinking. They just never picked up on the fact that the drink in front of him was always, always a mineral water. When they note his boisterousness, he typically jokes, "Imagine what I was like drunk!" In twenty-five years of conversations like that, he has almost never had anyone inquire in any depth about why he doesn't drink. Mostly, he doesn't offer and they don't ask.

The conviviality of the cocktail lounge is one factor. There's camaraderie in the cups. To be among your fellows, slightly sloshed, can be a lovely thing. There's also the flavor of a good stout, the elegance of a complex Bordeaux, or the nuance of a fine single malt scotch. There's the warm glow that comes like magic from just the right dose of alcohol.

Some will accuse us here of romanticizing alcohol and drugs. But it wouldn't be true to say that we were making these things up. Alcohol and, indeed, even drugs have played an enduring role in the unfolding drama of history. Champagne launched ships, cold beer has been a signal that the workday is done, and drinking wine, smoking marijuana, and eating hallucinogenic cactus have all been part of religious sacraments. None of these things are, in themselves, "bad." The alcoholic's problem is not that he drinks. It's that he *must* drink. Neither alcohol nor drugs need be deplored or demonized before you can choose to let them go. The decision to do so may be for you, as Shakespeare put it, sweet sorrow. Or you may make that choice simply because you feel it's time to leave the party. You don't have to make an enemy of drugs and alcohol to decide that it's time for you to stop using them for good—and we've already discussed some, we think, fairly compelling reasons you might want to do just that. Again, the choice rests with you. (We'll have more to say about this later on. The Two Paths Meditation from chapter 2 can be helpful in finding the space you need to make this kind of decision.)

Choosing Your Path

There are many paths to recovery from substance dependence. Some may tell you that there's only one way out of the trap of addiction. You must be saved in the _____ church (fill in your favorite religious tradition)! You must go to AA! You must knuckle down! You must go to treatment! And on and on. But if we could rewrite the universe of treatment, we would take pains to make it one with many alternatives.

There are many paths into and out of substance dependence. It's simply the case that many people have recovered without doing any of these things. And still many more people have failed to recover even while doing all of them. History is unquestionably filled with people who recovered with just a bit of friendly advice and no treatment at all. There are certainly people who just got up one morning and decided to let it go. But, if you were one of them, the chances are pretty low that you would have found your way to this book.

And while there are as many paths to recovery as there are people struggling with addiction who seek some other way of living, observation over time has suggested that some paths probably work better than others. We do know some things that predict whether people will have long-term substance problems. People with stable jobs and families and good strong social support have an easier time recovering, *on average*, than those who don't. People who start drinking or using later in life are more likely to recover, *on average*, than people who start earlier. People with fewer other psychological problems are more likely to recover and avoid relapse, *on average*, than people with more and more severe mental health issues. But even here, we need to point out that these things are true about groups of people *on average*. Some people keep drinking or using even though the cards are stacked in their favor, and some people recover with all the cards stacked against them.

And what about you? Which are you? Do you fit neatly into any of these categories? Or are you the exception to the averages? We don't know. At the risk of sounding like a broken record, we're not here to tell you whether you should abstain from drugs and alcohol. We have no particular opinion on that matter. We're libertarian enough to say that this is a matter for you—and only you—to decide. If, however, you've decided for yourself that it's time to let go of drugs and alcohol, if you find that drug and alcohol use is getting between you and a life that you could love, then we offer this book as a support in that task.

ACT as an Approach to Recovery

ACT is a behavioral treatment that has been shown to be useful with a wide variety of problems in living. There are clinical tests where ACT has been used with people who have problems with anxiety, depression, hallucinations, delusions, and chronic stress. ACT has been used with a lot of people struggling with different health problems like diabetes, chronic pain, obesity, and cancer. And, perhaps most important to you, ACT has been used successfully with a variety of addictions, including serious problems with multiple substances such as heroin, cocaine, and alcohol, with marijuana dependence, and with tobacco dependence. What's more, ACT self-help books have shown very good results in scientific tests.

Does this matter to you? It might, but we doubt it. And honestly, we don't think it should matter very much. Maybe you could be attracted to ACT's roots in science. Maybe it's appealing that the therapy has an expanding information base and practice community. Or maybe you're drawn to the fact that ACT has been applied to problems in many areas of life, not just a few. In the end, we believe that what really matters is whether what ACT has to offer resonates with you. And rather than go on and on about what ACT does have to offer, we'll put it all to you in one simple question:

In this very moment, will you accept the sad and the sweet, hold lightly stories about what is possible, and be the author of a life that has meaning and purpose for you, turning in kindness back to that life when you find yourself moving away from it?

From where we sit, this question, honestly and diligently answered, is the very heart of what ACT has to offer. It speaks to this very moment, to what is happening to you in your life, right here and right now. It asks you to accept that your life—everyone's life—is inevitably colored by things that are lovely and things that are painful. It reminds you that how you see the world right now might not necessarily be how things actually are and certainly doesn't determine how things might eventually become. It asks you what it is that you really want your life to be about and what you're willing to do to make it be so. And, finally, it asks if you are willing to commit, moment after moment after moment, to turn back to those things you value and care about, even when you've strayed—as we all do more often than we would like.

We'll have more to say about the particulars of ACT as we go along. For now, we invite you to sit for a moment with this question before reading on. It will matter a lot to the rest of the time you spend with us in this book.

So, now we begin our task. We invite you to give what we offer here a try. We'll be asking you to do some kind of crazy stuff: odd exercises, activities, meditations, writing assignments, and other sorts of things. It's our sincerest hope that you find things here that move you toward a life you can love.

2

IN THIS VERY MOMENT

Having spent the better part of my life trying to either relive the past or experience the future before it arrives, I have come to believe that in between these two extremes is peace.

—author unknown

What if there is as much living in a moment of pain as in a moment of joy? What if, right here in this very moment, peace is something you can enjoy? This chapter is about showing up in your own life and about the benefits of learning to practice the gift of stillness even in a storm, or maybe especially in a storm. The growing of such a practice can allow you to live with intention and purpose, even in the most trying moments that your life will surely deliver. If you're reading this book, we imagine such a resting place would be welcome.

Focusing on Yesterday and Tomorrow

We humans spend a lot of time going over and over the wrongs done by us or to us. Like cows, we chew and chew, but instead of chewing grass, we chew our troubles—over and over and over (and over and…well, you get the idea). Sometimes we worry about the future and what *might* happen. Sometimes we worry about whether the past will repeat itself. After that, we go over the long list of terrible things that just might happen. We fritter away precious moments trying to redo the irredeemable past and trying to fix the unknowable future.

Worrying is like spending time fussing over the road map in order to figure out traffic conditions miles ahead. The map just doesn't have much to offer in that area. (Yes, mobile technology and network-powered maps have changed this somewhat, but run with us on this one.) You might pick a less busy route, but if you spend a lot of time on the side of the road staring at a paper map, traffic conditions won't become any clearer to you. And, in the meantime, your progress on your journey stops. Another alternative is looking at the map while driving, but this kind of distraction has its own consequences (*Ahh!* Screams are heard from the back seat). Stopping on your journey to look at a map, momentarily, is a fine idea. But there's only so much the map can tell you. In order to get anywhere, you need to spend most of your trip traveling with your eyes on the road, watching for what will happen next. Ruminating is like spending all your time looking in the rearview mirror. Worrying about the future is like trying always to get a peek past the horizon while remaining oblivious to what's happening to you right now, at ground level. Sure, glance back and look far ahead sometimes—but doing nothing else is a surefire way to put your life in a ditch.

Worry and rumination as we understand them have one very significant thing in common, and it probably is very easy for you to figure out what that is: they both focus actively on some time other than right now. There is a promise buried in worry and rumination. The promise is that if we go over our mistakes thoroughly enough, if we worry out all the details of our future, we will somehow avoid future problems. Planning is important and so is reviewing the mistakes we've already made. But when planning and reviewing become full-time jobs, we miss out on a lot of things that are happening—right now.

You'll have no trouble at all, we think, in linking these not-now problems to your experience with substance abuse and recovery. It's likely that you remember a time when substance abuse wasn't an issue in your life, even if that time might have been when you were a child. And you probably spend a fair amount of time pondering the direction your life will take as time goes by. Will you stay sober or stop using? No one knows. No one can know, at least not as long as you keep breathing. Drinking or drug use is something that you can do as long as you have the freedom and independence to make your own decisions. But we're not going to talk now about whether or not you'll kick the stuff now or ever. Rather, our purpose in this chapter is to talk about the alternative to worry and rumination, to focusing actively on the future or the past. And that alternative is—you guessed it—focusing actively and flexibly on the present moment.

Common Sorts of Worry and Rumination

A very common source of worry in recovery is whether the recovery will last and whether the mess a person has made can ever be cleaned up. The biggest targets for rumination tend to be our past mistakes and, maybe to a lesser degree, the wrongs we perceive others have done to us.

"Will It Last?"

We mentioned this above, but it's such a huge deal in recovery for people who have decided to quit that it's more than worth repeating. From the moment you put down your glass, stub out your joint, or toss out your needles, no one can possibly know whether you'll drink or use again. This uncertainty is something you'll carry with you always, even after many years of sobriety, and it can be one of the most painful aspects of recovery.

There are a couple of ways people manage this uncertainty. One is forcefully expressing their certainty, telling anyone who will listen that they will never drink or use drugs again.

"I have really learned my lesson this time," they'll say. "Never again!"

They speak with authority and genuine conviction. They are committed to their objective. And they may succeed—or they may fail. There are plenty of "never again" stories that have unhappy endings. In fact, chances are very good that you've told yourself one version of this story or another.

I can't believe I did that. I will never get that drunk *again.* For a lot of us, the "that drunk" line had a habit of creeping until "that drunk" became a regular occurrence.

Why is this approach to managing the uncertainty about drinking or using so common? We think there are two reasons. First, we sincerely mean that we're done. We sincerely *intend* to quit drugs and alcohol permanently. And intentions *do* matter. The second reason, though, is more worrisome. We sometimes make these kinds of proclamations in order to suppress deep fears about relapse—but it's important to realize that suppressing fears can be a problem. There is very good science that shows harm caused by suppressing thoughts and emotions (Abramowitz, Tolin, and Street 2001). The saying goes: "What you resist persists." Also, it takes a lot of effort to suppress your fears, and we want you to spend your precious energy more profitably. Think of effort as a personal investment. This book is about helping you invest in your life, not in some crummy thought. We will be talking about some very specific ways to do that as we go along.

There is only one way to truly know if recovery will last. There is only one way to completely and absolutely end the scariness of not knowing. Drink. If you drink, you will know it will not last. This may sound crazy, but it has happened many, many times. Consider:

Bob gets sober. Things start to get on track. It is the first time in years that things have gone this well. Bob trumpets: "This time I have really learned my lesson. This time quitting is for good." But there is a little seed of doubt in there. In the wee hours of the night, when everyone else is asleep, Bob's mind starts talking to him. *Sure Bob*, it says. *Sure. But that's what you said last time.* Bob has a little debate in his head and doesn't get much sleep that night.

Slowly, these little seeds of doubt start to show up in Bob's everyday life. An emotional situation comes up with his ex-wife. Out of the blue, the thought shows up, *A drink would be good right about now.* Bob is shocked and says to himself, *Never, never, never!* But later that night, while the world is fast asleep, Bob wakes up. His mind says, *One drink, Bob. What harm can that do?* "No," says Bob, out loud this time. *Someday,* says Bob's mind. *Someday.*

Before long, this argument is plaguing Bob day and night. *Will I, won't I? Will I, won't I?* Over and over and over, along with all of the reasons yes and all of the reasons no. Bob fights and fights. Some days it feels like Bob's head is going to explode. Bob can feel a tightness in his chest almost as if his muscles are about to break his ribs. Bob starts snapping at people at work. Someone makes a wisecrack: "Wow, Bob! I think I liked you better drunk."

And it builds and builds until Bob thinks he just cannot stand another second of the pressure. Bob knows that he can't keep this up. Maybe for a day or a week or even a month. Next month? Maybe, maybe not. But forever? No.

And then what will happen? To my job, my kids, my house?

Bob knows that eventually he will crack. He may be able to keep it up for a day or a week or maybe even a month, but forever? There is no chance he can keep this up forever. One day, in a rush, Bob pops open a bottle and takes a long, slow draw. And for a moment, Bob knows peace. All that uncertainty is washed away. Bob's skin fits better. Bob has room to breathe. A guy has to breathe, after all.

The problem is that the space Bob bought with the drink evaporates like rain on a summer sidewalk. Bob would not be on the merry-go-round with drinking if the relief were still working for him.

"My God! What Have I Done!?"

In recovery, a very common worry is about whether you will relapse. The most common subjects for rumination, though, are the mistakes of your past. You know they can't be undone. Can amends be made? Will you be forgiven? Can you (maybe) forgive? For some of us, the most painful memories from our past have been associated with drinking or drug use. Our darkest nights, our most devastating losses can be traced to ill-conceived moments that may have started in the bottom of a bottle or at the tip of a needle.

Here's what we assume—not what we know, because the future cannot truly be known. We assume that no matter what you've done and no matter what has happened to you, you can build a life that is rich and meaningful. We assume that no matter where you've been in your life, even if you are reading this book on death row, you can make a life about which, at the end of your days, you can say, "Yes, that life, that living, was mine, and I am grateful to have had it." Fundamentally, this entire book in dedicated to the service of that aim.

The point of the whole story about Bob is that as long as Bob is busy grinding over the past and future, he is less effective today. So, how do we let it go and find our way to the here and now?

People get smacked around in life. It's inevitable. You just have to have enough birthdays, and you'll take a beating. (And for some of us, the worst beatings came at our own hands.) When we humans take a beating, we have a few basic moves. We hide. We run. We fight. There's a problem, though. When you have your hands balled into fists, it is hard to pick up a baby or a flower or a book of poetry. When your hands are covering your ears or eyes, you can't even hear or see what's available to you. And likewise, it's hard to see much of anything with clarity when you are running at full speed.

We humans spend a lot of time hiding, running, and fighting. Using drugs and alcohol is the preferred way of hiding and running for some of us. It seems like it gets the job done. A stiff drink can sometimes go a long way toward fighting off the blues, at least for a while. It's a scary thing to let go of hiding, and fighting, and running—perversely because one of the first things you are likely to see when you do let go is all the damage that has been caused by hiding, fighting, and running.

When you are hiding, fighting, and running, there are two things that really capture your awareness. One of these is the thing you don't like. The other is the exit, the way out (or, at least, what seems to be the way out). Think of it this way: if you were in a department store and a lion walked in the door, you would be aware of the lion. That's for sure. And you would also become keenly aware of the nearest exit—or you'd be in a damned big hurry to find it if it wasn't readily apparent. You would probably not be particularly aware of the color of the carpet, which set of flatware was on sale, or whether this season's jeans were tending to be mid- or low-rise.

Running from your past or your future or from yourself works the same way (though it is not at all clear which way to turn!), and the same is true for fighting and hiding. All these efforts cause you to be less present in your own life. This chapter has two central purposes. One is to go to work on the general skill of showing up and staying present. The other is the more particular task of making contact with the place you find yourself in this very moment. We will aim to bring these two things together and then carry them forward into the rest of our work together.

The Ubiquity of Suffering

Of course, all the creatures of the earth get smacked around one way or another, but humans have some special suffering that is reserved just for us. There is a joke we know, sort of dark humor. The joke goes: What is the difference between a dog and a human?

The answer goes like this: You kick a dog and a human out of a nice warm house into a rainstorm, and then later you let them both come back inside. The human stands by the door, shivering and dripping all over the floor, wondering why he got thrown out, going over what led up to it, raging about how unfairly he was treated, thinking he didn't deserve it, plotting revenge on the person who threw him out, worrying whether he'll be thrown out again, wracking his brain to decide whether the neighbors will take him in, and generally imagining a world in which he spends most of his time outside in the cold, cold rain. Meanwhile, the dog is sound asleep in front of the fire, his paws jerking a little now and then as he chases birds and rabbits through his canine dreamscape.

Humans do not just suffer. Suffering, for us, is ubiquitous—it's an all-day, every-day, and any-place kind of condition. We suffer that we have suffered in the past, and we suffer that we might suffer in the future. No matter where we are, there is a where-we-are-not that is better than where we are. There is a before that we wish we could go back to or a later we wish we could skip ahead to. And, if right now is perfect, we worry that it will not last. Coming to stillness, coming to rest, is always for later, as soon as we _____. Just fill in the blank with whatever conditions have to be met in your own life. The problem is that the time seems never to come. There's always something just waiting to fill in that blank.

We're proposing something different here than waiting for life to deliver just the right time and circumstance. What if you could find the wherewithal to act in the fashion of your choosing any place, at any time, regardless of preexisting conditions or any guaranteed outcome? We think it's possible, although there is a big catch. If you're still and composed in this very moment, there's very little that you can't initiate from within it. But stillness is hard-won. Our goal here is to help you foster the ability to claim stillness. We think stillness can be both a gift and a skill.

Here is how Kipling said it:

If

If you can keep your head when all about you
Are losing theirs and blaming it on you,
If you can trust yourself when all men doubt you,
But make allowance for their doubting too;
If you can wait and not be tired by waiting,
Or being lied about, don't deal in lies,
Or being hated, don't give way to hating,
And yet don't look too good, nor talk too wise:

If you can dream—and not make dreams your master;
If you can think—and not make thoughts your aim;
If you can meet with Triumph and Disaster
And treat those two impostors just the same;
If you can bear to hear the truth you've spoken
Twisted by knaves to make a trap for fools,
Or watch the things you gave your life to broken,
And stoop and build 'em up with wornout tools:

If you can make one heap of all your winnings
And risk it on one turn of pitch-and-toss,
And lose, and start again at your beginnings
And never breathe a word about your loss;
If you can force your heart and nerve and sinew
To serve your turn long after they are gone,
And so hold on when there is nothing in you
Except the Will which says to them: "Hold on!"

If you can talk with crowds and keep your virtue,
Or walk with kings—nor lose the common touch,
If neither foes nor loving friends can hurt you,
If all men count with you, but none too much;
If you can fill the unforgiving minute
With sixty seconds' worth of distance run—

> Yours is the Earth and everything that's in it,
> And—which is more—you'll be a Man my son!

(Rudyard Kipling, 1895)

We are going to grow your stillness muscle through practice. We will especially want to have stillness available in a storm, so we'll ask you to invite some storms and then practice stillness while in their midst.

Stillness and the Inclined Heart

In the next section, we're going to introduce part 1 of an inventory of drug and alcohol use and the fallout from that use. The inventory is a place to practice. The inventory is a place to build your stillness muscle. You will need that muscle later. Before we introduce it, we want to introduce the idea of *the inclined heart*. We first found the metaphor of the inclined heart in the work of Jon Kabat-Zinn (2006), whose work we both admire and respect. If you come at the inventory running, hiding, and fighting, the work you do with it will likely do you little good. There is an alternative, though. You can approach the inventory in stillness and with your heart inclined toward it. Imagine if your heart were like a bowl. If that bowl were held upright and covered, nothing would spill from it and nothing would flow into it. But imagine that you could uncover your heart and gently incline it toward different people and experiences in your own life. This is easy to do with things we love. It's much harder to do with things that we are mad about or ashamed of. But if you can incline your heart toward hard things, you can let some of what's there flow into the world, and you can take something back. And this is a part of moving forward that we believe is very important.

Have you approached things in your life with a closed heart? Do you know the cost of that? As you do the inventory that follows, stop occasionally. Allow yourself to go still, even for just a moment. Picture your own heart as a bowl. Imagine pulling the cover from it and inclining it toward the different parts of the inventory. If you have any trouble at all picturing a bowl, get an actual bowl and keep it handy. The problem with keeping your heart covered is that sealing out pain often also means sealing out love. We know that some areas will be hard, but try it and see what happens.

◂ Practicing Our Way to the Gift of Stillness— Part 1

In this inventory, we'll ask you to see if you can start to notice places in your life where you have been absent or perhaps less present in some way. See if you can let go of self-condemnation for now. You can always condemn yourself later. There'll be plenty of time for that if you decide later on that you need to give yourself a beating. For now, though, let this be more like an exercise in noticing.

Below you'll find a list of twelve aspects of life. Some may be important to you, and some may not. That's fine. These are areas of living that some people care about. Let your eyes come to rest on each one.

- ‣ Family (other than your spouse or partner and your children)

- ‣ Marriage and intimate relationships

- ‣ Parenting

- ‣ Friends / social life

- ‣ Work

- ‣ Education and learning

- ‣ Recreation and fun

- ‣ Spirituality

- ‣ Community life

- ‣ Physical care, exercise, sleep, nutrition

- ‣ The environment and nature

- ‣ Art, music, literature, and beauty

We're going to invite you to reflect on some of these areas. You can do all twelve, if you like, but we recommend starting with only three or four that resonate with you the most.

Let yourself become aware of the first area you choose to reflect on. Slowly, gently allow yourself to become aware of ways you've been absent, of times when you could have been present to this area of your life and just weren't. Don't judge or evaluate. Just notice.

You may not be able to think of any examples of not showing up that related to a particular area. That's fine. This is an inventory. There are no right or wrong answers, and the whole exercise isn't about *doing* anything. It is about learning how to notice and to gently shift your attention. Ultimately, it's about learning how to be still. See if you can bring your gentlest "you" to the task.

When you're ready, move on to the next area you want to reflect on. Take your time. Slow down. Breathe. There is nothing to accomplish here, nothing to be done other than to notice and ponder. You've struggled enough. For now, for right now, see if you can take that cover off your heart and incline it in the direction of these hard thoughts. If something is going to flow in, let it. If something is going to spill out, that's fine. Whatever happens, breathe through it and let yourself come to rest.

◂

◂ Six Breaths on Purpose

Here's a little tip. If you find yourself caught in an old pattern of worry or rumination, stop for a moment, let your eyes go closed, and notice the sensation of the rise and fall of breath. Take six long, slow, deliberate breaths and then gently turn your attention back to the inventory. Do this as many times as you find your attention hooked by some thought storm. These moments are not obstacles. They are opportunities to practice coming to stillness. The more times they happen, the more practice you will get. That is a good thing.

◂

Self-help books like to give a lot of examples, especially when it comes to completing exercises. This isn't really our thing. If we start to write about how "Bob let himself go quiet and allowed his attention to move toward his love of sports, in particular baseball, and all the games he missed because he was spending his afternoons at the bar…" it seems pretty evident to us that you, too, will start thinking about your relationship to baseball or some other sport, and that's not really the point. We want to create an opportunity here for you to practice stillness with this exercise, and we're confident that you can figure out what each area means to you. That said, there are a few kinds of not-showing-up that are pretty common and that are related in a particular way to the problems of drinking and drug use.

Ways to Not Show Up

When you're invited to a party that you really don't want to attend, you might RSVP that you will come and then, simply, not show up. In this case, you're removing yourself physically from a situation that you find unpleasant for some reason. Your not-showing-up is very literal. This, of course, is one kind of not showing up. And it's not necessarily a bad thing. Skipping a dreadful party full of bores so you can go walk in the forest, swim in the sea, or do something else that matters to you is a fine idea. But when what you really want to do is actually go to the party and have a good time, not-showing-up becomes a problem. More precisely, it's a problem of avoidance. If you find your mind wandering, use Six Breaths on Purpose and then return to the task.

Not all kinds of not-showing-up are literal. Have you ever found yourself driving down the highway when your attention suddenly snaps back to the road in front of you and you realize you have no idea what has happened for the last however-many miles because your head was someplace else? It's an example of not-showing-up that happens when you are definitely physically present in the driver's seat. Probably more often than not, we figure out ways to be in the room without *really* being in the room.

Fighting

You have to be present to fight, right? Not really. Your words or your fists can be flying while what's really going on is anything but your active engagement in the conflict in front of you. Being in conflict and arguing can lead us to focus on "winning" in relationships, at great cost to the health of those same relationships. Is the objective you're fighting for a primary goal for you? Or is it a distraction—a dodge that buys you a little space from the real issue, the real source of hurt? Getting into fights can give you something to feel busy about, something to distract you from scarier, more painful things that can get lost in the tussle and roar of the fight. Are you a fighter? Can you name some things you may have missed while in the middle of the fight?

Another version of fighting is reason-giving and being right. When we feel blamed or judged by others and also by ourselves, we fight against the condemnation with reasons. Are you a reason-giver? While you have been busy giving reasons, are there things you have ignored or not noticed? We are not concerned here with whether the reasons are true or false. Arguing about "true" reasons can cause us to miss things just as much as arguing about "false" reasons. The focus here is on noticing the things that get lost while defending the reasons—true or false though they may be.

Running and Hiding

With wild animals it is pretty easy to see the difference between running and hiding. The mouse hides. If you discover its hiding place, it runs. Both serve the same purpose. They keep the mouse safe. It is a little trickier to tell the difference with humans. Just like fighting, running and hiding are ways to protect ourselves. So, using the example of relationships again: have you been hiding or running? Maybe you literally hide—you stay home in your apartment or avoid answering the phone. Or maybe you hide inside even when it does not look like you are hiding from the outside. Some people look like the life of the party. They have a public face and a private face that are very different, and when they are in a crowd, they feel alone. They have thoughts like: *People don't really know me—they only know the me I let them see.*

For many of us, drinking and using are the primary methods of running and hiding. Alcohol and drugs are also the source of a lot of fights. If the idea of not-showing-up didn't click for you when you started the inventory, how do you feel about it now? Can you think of times when not-showing-up for you looked like a fight, like reason-giving, or like running and hiding? If you like, go back through each area and note any additional ways you might have used drugs or alcohol that made you less present.

◄ PRACTICING OUR WAY TO THE GIFT OF STILLNESS— PART 2

Before we go on in our inventory, we want to remind you that this isn't an exercise in "what's wrong with me." That sort of thought may well be called up as you fill the inventory out, and we want you—surprise, surprise—to allow yourself to show up for that thought, even if it's very hard to bear. Remember that our purpose here is to help you start to practice pausing, to practice coming to stillness when hard things are in front of you. Learn to notice any tendencies you have to hide, run, or fight when things get ugly.

Hiding may sound like: *I don't need to do this.* Running may sound like: *I'll do this later.* Fighting may sound like: *Why do I need to do this?! You can't make me do this!* That's all true: you don't need to do this work at all, and you can certainly put this work off until later, and we absolutely can't make you do anything. But if you can learn to slow down and to pause in the face of hard things, you will be better practiced at pausing later on when we start talking about taking a direction, about choosing a path.

To continue this inventory, we want you to go back over the areas you just reflected upon. Call each of them to mind. Allow your eyes to go closed. And when you're ready, ponder each of these three questions in relation to that area of your life.

- What does this area mean to you?

- What would you hope for it to mean?

- In a world where you could take time, in a world where you could offer yourself a gift in this area, what gift might you offer?

After practicing a few moments of noticing in stillness in these areas, write a bit about each question. Write down a few specific examples if you can think of a few.

The last question is especially important. It starts to point you in the direction of what you want your life to be about. Maybe you can't have everything you can imagine. Maybe some things really aren't possible for you. But if you're willing to give yourself one small gift in any area of your life that matters to you, you start down a path that can lead to a richer, more fulfilling life.

The Day Weariness Became Your Best Friend

How hard it is to find that still place when your heart and mind are pulling you every which way? Pretty damned hard, right? And even though I've been telling you that finding that moment of stillness is important for some reason, you're well within your rights to think I'm out of my mind. You've been drinking or using to get away from that kind of pain. You *need* to get away from that pain.

Or do you?

How has it worked for you to always need to get away from the pain? To need to run from the hard things? To live with a barricade up between your heart and what was out there to hurt it? The nasty secret is that the hard stuff doesn't wait for an opening. It finds its way in like cold winter air through whatever cracks it can find—and there are always cracks.

Living with your heart closed hurts. Living with your heart open hurts too. Why go to the bother? I think it might be because you're tired. Tired and dragging and looking for someplace, anyplace you can come to rest.

Your best friend at this moment may be your own weariness. Are you tired? Tired of running, hiding, fighting? Let this book be a place to come to rest. I'm begging you. On my knees. Really. I've certainly been on my knees for less dignified reasons. Let this book be an invitation to come to rest. Let this book be an invitation to a life lived with heart wide open.

Living with an open heart takes practice—persistent practice. In some respects, this practice is described throughout this book. If you open your hands, your arms, your head, your heart, certain things will fall into your hands. Some days, what falls into my hands looks, feels, and smells like shit. I'm asking you, throughout this book, whether you're willing to open your arms and, from time to time, to catch an armload of shit. And rather than say you have to be willing to do that, I'm trying to show you that your willingness to let in the bad things leaves you open to good and wonderful and beautiful things as well. Consider for a moment if maybe, just maybe, this invitation could lead you to have things fall into your open arms and your open heart that you cannot even imagine. (And maybe you have found that you end up with more than just the occasional armload of shit anyway—no matter how closed you are, no matter how well you hide, no matter how hard you fight, and no matter how fast you run.)

Let this book be an invitation to live a life with heart wide open. You can always go back to what you have been doing if you are not satisfied. It might sound impossible, but for now, let's just hold it as a possibility. If you feel uncertain about that, excellent! You are right where you are supposed to be. Possibility and uncertainty always hang out together. Welcome.

The Fear of Uncertainty

Human beings are not wired to like uncertainty. We evolved out on the savanna and it was dangerous out there. There were lions and tigers and bears. The careless were eaten. We learned quickly what to be afraid of. We stayed away from places the lions, tigers, and bears went. But we learned something else too. We learned to stay away from places the lions, tigers, and bears *might* go, or have ever been, or might ever think of going, and so forth.

Struggling to Make the World Safe and Certain

The world is a place of constant change, yet we want the world to hold still and behave. The problem for humans is that there is always a where-you-are-not that's better than where you are or a where-you-were that's better than where you are. And if where you are is just right, watch out, because that little fantasy house of cards can all come crashing down at any moment. And so we struggle to avoid suffering.

But that struggle is inevitably in vain. It recalls the old Buddhist parable in which a young woman's only child dies. She runs from house to house, asking her neighbors for help in resurrecting her boy. One after the other they turn her away, until finally one neighbor tells her to go ask the Buddha for help. She does, and the Buddha tells her he will revive her child. His price? A handful of mustard seed. The young woman is delighted. But, the Buddha tells her, there is a catch: the mustard seeds must come from the garden of a family in which no one had lost a child, spouse, parent, or friend.

Once we're born into this world, we will lose everything we love and care about until, one day, we ourselves will die, despite every action we might take to the contrary. Our efforts to avoid this kind of suffering can provide temporary relief, but there is no getting away from the fact that we will, certainly, suffer. Drinking and using drugs can offer temporary escape. In an uncertain world, drink and drugs can provide a bit of the illusion of certainty, but for some of us, the cost of that certainty is too high.

Uncertainty and Change

Our deep concern with uncertainty is also why we do not like change. Anytime there is a change, we might rightly wonder how the change will go. Change contains uncertainty. Where we are might not be great, but it is known. The thinking goes, *I may be in a rut, but it is my rut. I have been here a while. I have put down a nice carpet and hung a few pictures on the walls. It may not be much, but it is familiar.*

Stepping outside our comfort zone involves a decidedly uncertain walk. People have a couple of approaches to that uncertainty. One is to stay in their rut, or, to retreat back to it at any sign of trouble. Another is to leap into discomfort and change—like jumping from a high dive. Recovery is like that. Some tread around the edges—falling in and out. Some leap in with the fever of a new convert. We are suggesting another path. Something gentler, kinder, more thoughtful, with eyes open and choices made one by one—taking you in a direction that has a sense of rightness to it, even though you are not certain exactly where the path will lead. Robert Frost said it well.

The Road Not Taken

Two roads diverged in a yellow wood,
And sorry that I could not travel both
And be one traveler, long I stood
And looked down one as far as I could
To where it bent in the undergrowth;

Then took the other, as just as fair,
And having perhaps the better claim,
Because it was grassy and wanted wear
Though as for that the passing there
Had worn them really about the same.

And both that morning equally lay
In leaves no step had trodden black.
Oh, I kept the first for another day!
Yet knowing how way leads onto way,
I doubted if I should ever come back.

I shall be telling this with a sigh
Somewhere ages and ages hence:
Two roads diverged in a yellow wood, and I—
I took the one less traveled by,
And that has made all the difference.

(Robert Frost, 1920)

And you, my friend: in this very moment, what paths lie before you? And which will you take on this day?

◄ The Two Paths Meditation: Pausing at the Junction of Two Paths in the Woods

Let us stop for just a moment here and imagine that your life is like that walk in the woods described by Frost. Could it be that we are truly always at that junction—at every single moment of our lives? Could it be that we could stop at any moment and see different paths we might take? If we could pause as a choice as we moved through our day, what an asset that would be!

So now,

Right now,

Right at this very moment,

Let us stop

And practice stopping,

And seeing,

In hope that this practice will serve us in the days to come.

Let us stop together for a moment and let ourselves see the paths that lie before us. Set a timer for five minutes. Allow yourself to settle into a comfortable seated posture. Allow your eyes to go gently closed or your focus to soften. Take Six Breaths on Purpose and just let go of everything. Make a friend of your own breath. Notice its gentle rise and fall through five or six cycles. Notice the temperature of the breath and the sensations in the body as the chest and belly rise and fall. Practice taking good deep breaths, filling your lungs slowly and completely and emptying them slowly and completely, and, with each, letting your breath become your friend. Let your breath become a place you can come to stillness. Imagine that your breath could offer you the gift of stillness.

After settling into your breath, imagine that you stand at a point where two paths separate before you. Let yourself see the paths, and let yourself be uncertain about where the paths lead. Let yourself wonder. Imagine that you could lean forward slightly so that you were at the point of tipping toward one path or the other. If you find yourself being certain about which path, see if you can let go of that certainty for just a few minutes and allow yourself to stay inside the question, to stay inside the uncertainty.

◀

Making Friends with Uncertainty

Why make friends with uncertainty? *What if uncertainty and possibility live in the same house?* What if the price of possibility is making friends with uncertainty? It is hard to take, but it seems to be the case. If you look around at the things you care most about in life, you will find uncertainty. How will this marriage go? How will having children go? How will this career choice go? All contain a lot of uncertainty. Making friends with uncertainty means that you get to go places that are unknown to you. If you are entirely satisfied with where life has taken you, this matters little. But if you have a longing for more, come along.

Missing Things

We could ask the question in only one way—"How has life been going?"—but there is a problem with asking in that way. We remember some things, but not others. Think about your own childhood. If you are like most of us, you remember bits and pieces, snapshots, a select number of particularly good times, and perhaps particularly bad. But remembering the fifth year of your life will not be like replaying the fifth song on your favorite CD.

Sometimes memory selects in a negative way—all we can see is what is wrong. Sometimes it selects in a positive way—big problems lurk all around us unnoticed. Later we may say to ourselves: *How did I miss that?!* Here is how: you are human. It is simply part of the human condition to miss things. Missing things is not a bad thing, except when it is.

Stopping to Smell the Roses

There are a thousand stories, songs, and poems that remind us to stop and smell the roses. If missing things were not so common, there would not be so many songs and poems.

Sometimes we miss things because we move by them too quickly or move by them looking from a particular vantage point. Think of a place you have driven many times. If I asked you what was along the way, you would not be able to tell me every stone, stick, and pebble along the way. There is no need to. You need to know where the gas stations and the grocery store are, and you might also know some things that matter little. However, you could stop anywhere along that road, sit down, look, listen, and smell, and you would see, hear, and smell things you have never known—even though you had passed that spot a hundred times.

Try it in your own house. What we are about to ask you to do is weird, but humor us.

◀ SEEING WHAT'S THERE

Part 1: Get up and walk from wherever you are reading to a bedroom or some other room. When you come back, go to the bottom of page 35 in this book and follow the instructions.

Part 2: Start walking from your living room to your bedroom again. Count to five and then, wherever you happen to be, stop. Lie down on the floor on your side. (We warned you that we were going to ask you to do weird things.) Let your head come to rest on the floor. Allow yourself to relax and just open up all your senses. Let your eyes go closed and just listen for the smallest sounds. Notice temperature. Notice smells. Let your eyes come gently open and look around. Again, take in the details. Just allow yourself to get quiet, relax, and take it in.

- See: Start by looking around from that perspective. Spend a couple of minutes. Be patient. Notice, especially, color, light, and detail. I just tried this and I noticed the bathroom door is slightly lower on the hinge side. There are several small cracks in the baseboard. There are small aluminum hinges on the bottom of the furnace air return. I could see a huge variety of colors in the hardwood floor—reds, browns, yellows, in very soft subtle shades.

- Hear: I listened and the main sound was the furnace running. It started out sounding like one sound but as I listened for a minute, within that sound there was a sort of cycling from higher to lower sounds. There were little ticking sounds in there. If I listened carefully, I could barely hear the sound of the refrigerator running in the other room.

- Feel: I could feel the cool of the floor on my cheek. I could feel the grain in the hardwood floor. I could reach out and feel the texture of the paint on the wall. As I got quiet and settled in, I started to notice the feel of different parts of my body that touched and did not touch the floor.

- Smell: There was a cool wood smell.

If you do this you may see, hear, feel, and smell things that you never noticed before. The reason is the pace. You would have noticed different things if I had asked you to walk briskly down the hall.

Try this same exercise other places in your life. You do not have to lie on the floor to do the exercise. You can do this noticing anywhere. Stop and stand on a street corner and try the same thing. Stop in the cafeteria at work. Try it riding on the bus to work. Lie down in the grass at the park. Practice coming to stillness and noticing. Grow your stillness muscle.

◀

Let's keep going with the inventory idea we started earlier in the chapter. Now you won't be reflecting on areas of your life. Instead, you'll be recalling and writing down a history of your alcohol and drug use. As you do this piece of work, we invite you to pause every so often and do the Two Paths Meditation. Let your eyes go closed. Settle into an appreciation of your own breath. See the paths. Let yourself come to stillness in the midst of wondering where the paths might take you. Then open your eyes again and go gently back to the inventory. Let the inventory itself be a sort of meditation.

Right now, we are not problem solving. We are surveying. Problem solving will be for later. You may come up with a lot of self-talk about how to solve the problems you see or how impossible they are. For now, we'll ask that you let go of problem solving. For now, we'll ask you to let go of conversations about what's possible and impossible. We'll rejoin those conversations later—we promise. If you find your head filled with words like always, never, must, can't, should, shouldn't, possible, or impossible, it's time for a break and a few minutes with the Two Paths Meditation or Six Breaths on Purpose.

◄ Practicing Our Way to the Gift of Stillness— Part 3

In a notebook, for any of the substances mentioned below that apply, write down:

- The age you started using

- How long you used

- The frequency of use (in times per week, month, or whatnot)

- How you used the substance (smoked, drank, ate, injected, and so forth)

Include a section for each category and an entry for each of the following substances that you've used:

- Alcohol

- Marijuana

- Hallucinogens (LSD, mushrooms, peyote, and so forth)

- Depressants (Xanax, valium, barbiturates, and so forth)

- Stimulants (speed, cocaine, ecstasy, ephedrine, and so forth)

- Inhalants (glue, gasoline, aerosol propellants, and so forth)

- Opiates (heroin, Vicodin, codeine, Oxycontin, Percodan, and so forth)

Begin with the first time you remember using any mood-altering substance, no matter how little of the substance you used. It is important that you be painstakingly thorough in this task. You can use a format like the one in the sample below or just write a description of your age and usage pattern.

Example: Stimulants

Age	Quantity/Frequency	How Used
12 yrs to 15 yrs	amphetamines 2–3 tablets / 6–8 X per year	oral
16 yrs	a few lines of cocaine/about 4 X that year	snorted
17 yrs	about 1/4 gram of cocaine/about 3–6 X per week	snorted, some smoked

Substance Inventory

Age	Quantity/Frequency	How Used
16	Vodka, mixed drinks weekends intermittently (experienced reg. blackouts)	drank
18	Liquor, mixed drinks, wine, week days + weekends, cocaine	drank, snorted
20–21, 22–23	Same as above, daily drinking, LSD, mushrooms	drank, oral (2-3x)
24–26 27 ⟶	Daily alcohol use started attempting sobriety	drank
28–31	Weekly drinking (4-5x/wk) rather than daily	◄
32	mostly sober (1 year)	

*22 – 1st sober attempt

* Instructions for Seeing What's There exercise: Write down what you saw, heard, felt, and smelled as you made that walk.

This may well seem like a long and difficult task. For many of us it is. It really is doable though. Just pick a substance and work your way through from first use to present. Take your time. If you find yourself unable to remember for one substance or time period, switch to another and work on that for a while. Sometimes working on another area will help you remember more about the one you are having trouble with. If, in the end, you find that you simply cannot remember for certain substances or time periods, make your best estimate. Remember, pause frequently and use Six Breaths on Purpose or the Two Paths Meditation. The inventory is about learning to pause, so pause.

◀ PRACTICING OUR WAY TO THE GIFT OF STILLNESS— PART 4

Okay, ready for part 4? This section should be done after you've done the first three parts. Write down any problems or changes in your life that were associated with using alcohol or drugs in each of the listed areas. In some ways this is a slightly harder look than the look we made at these areas in part 1. In part 1, we were just looking for general ways you might have been less than fully present. For a lot of us, drugs and alcohol were an important way to check out. If that is true, there are likely to have been consequences. Those consequences are what you're going to reflect on in part 4.

Appreciating in Sadness Certain Consequences and Turning Points

Sometimes consequences do not seem that bad at the time, but they signal later shifts that were more important. For example, I had a best friend in school from about the fourth grade up into high school. My first recollection of Sonny was on the playground. I was small for my age and nerdy—with big black glasses. Sonny was a big athletic kid with a huge heart. He was sort of a protector for me all through elementary and middle school. He was my best friend.

When I was about fifteen years old and had begun smoking pot, Sonny confronted me one night about my having offered his girlfriend some pot. He warned me to stay away from him and from her. I think I could see the sadness of that in his eyes at the time, just the other side of the warning. That night, I shrugged it off. They were square and I was….er, well, I guess I thought I was pretty cool. I recall telling the story to my pals in a way that made him seem unhip and me very cool and collected. In retrospect, there was a shift under way. I was shifting away from the people I had grown up with and in the direction of a crowd that was drinking and getting high. The deed was not done on the night Sonny warned me off, but that event remains in memory, and it saddens me.

I think there was considerable pain for Sonny, saying goodbye to his best pal. And me, I treated it as if it were something to be laughed off. It was a single friend lost, but it marked a much larger shift in my life. And to you, my old friend Sonny, my friend in whose presence I was always safe: I feel sad and sorry that I treated our friendship in such a careless way.

If there were no consequences, write none. However, we would encourage you to list consequences even though they may have been small. For example, you may not have been fired from a job, but you may have gone to work with a hangover and been less effective as a result. This need not have been ineffectiveness that others noticed. What is important is your own sense of this. Number each section and keep the twelve areas separate from each other as much as possible. What we're looking for here is any cost of using. It is absolutely okay to be repetitive. In fact, repetition is quite common and worth noticing. Pay special attention to places where, as result of drinking or using (or drug seeking), you did things that violate your personal values (concealing, rationalizing, being secretive, being violent, etc.). The inventory does not need to be exhaustive. Who could remember everything? And, why? Instead just give a few very specific examples in each section. Here are the areas again.

- Family (other than your spouse or partner and your children)

- Marriage and intimate relationships

- Parenting

- Friends / social life

- Work

- Education and learning

- Recreation and fun

- Spirituality

- Community life

- Physical care, exercise, sleep, nutrition

- The environment and nature

- Art, music, literature, and beauty

FROM NOT NOW TO...WHAT COMES NEXT
RELATING THE GIFT OF STILLNESS IN ACT TO AA

You will find lots of places where practicing stillness will serve you in AA. Some of the obvious places are where the program suggests prayer and meditation. Prayer and meditation are in the eleventh step, which calls for prayer and meditation and a regular practice of taking time from your day to become aware of your life direction. Many in AA use a book like *As Bill Sees It* or *Daily Reflections*. You could also choose something from a spiritual or philosophical tradition that resonates with you, like the Bible or the Dao De Jing. Just as stopping to stretch can be a good way to begin exercise, taking a few minutes in stillness after reading a short recovery-relevant or spiritual passage can be a great way to begin the day. You do not have to wait for the eleventh step to begin this practice. Today would be a good day to start. Sometimes the business of the day carries us off without our getting centered and reflecting on our intentions for the day. We invite you to take time now for reflection and stillness and setting of an intention for this day.

Equally critical is learning to practice stillness in the midst of a storm. The inventories in this chapter link up very closely with several of the 12 steps. The first step involves an admission of the true costs of drinking and using. The fourth-step inventory looks more systematically at these costs. In the AA Big Book (as the book *Alcoholics Anonymous* [2008] is popularly known), it is called a fearless and searching moral inventory, which sounds pretty menacing. But really, it is just a stock-taking. The inventories are not intended as yet another opportunity for beating yourself up. If taking a beating was all that was needed to "cure" alcoholism and addiction and the bad behavior that often accompany them, there would not be any addicts or alcoholics. Heaven knows you have likely taken a lot of beatings on your way to this book—probably many delivered from you to you. This is why in these inventories, you can focus on stillness and the inclined heart. We believe that to be the intention of the first, fourth, and ninth steps, which involve careful self-examination. Here is how they put it in AA's 12 & 12 (*Twelve Steps and Twelve Traditions* [1981]): "There is a direct linkage among self-examination, meditation, and prayer. Taken separately, these practices can bring much relief and benefit. But when they are logically related and interwoven, the result is an unshakeable foundation for life." (12 & 12, 98). This is exactly what we are trying to accomplish in the inventories in this and other chapters of this book.

Really, the idea of pausing and coming to stillness within significant questions can be found throughout the steps. You might ask yourself in the midst of the second step: *Might I come to believe that a power greater than myself could restore some semblance of good order to my life?* In fact, if the word "God" grates on you, you could follow the practice of those members of AA who call God "Good Orderly Direction." Some have used the group as a higher power and a source of direction. Some have said God is good. What if coming to believe simply meant allowing the "good" in your own life to organize what you do with your hours and days? If you are spiritually inclined, you will find many prayers throughout the Big Book. We encourage you to practice stillness, even for just a few moments, in the midst of the various prayers. If you are not so spiritually inclined, consider adding one little "o" to the prayers. Consider the impact of adding a single "o" to the AA third step: "Made a decision to turn our will and our lives over to the care of Good as we understood It." The third step is about a regular practice of aligning yourself with some sense of good direction. We will say more about this later, in our chapter on values. Practice at stillness, when stillness is easy and when stillness is hard, will be an asset.

Another place you can practice stillness will be in 12-step meetings. Like everywhere else in the world, if you go to meetings you will hear some real jerks. You are likely to get steamed listening to them. You might want to argue, but there is no crosstalk in 12-step meetings. Each person who speaks generally gets to do so uninterrupted. Since you can't respond out loud, you may be tempted to engage in the argument in your head. And, while you are busy off in your head grinding over the things that person said, you can become so distracted that you lose the rest of the meeting.

We encourage you to practice stillness in these circumstances. Try Six Breaths on Purpose and bring your intention back to the meeting. There is likely to be at least one jerk in every meeting. Think of it this way: unless you are a saint, one day that one jerk may be you. You may come into a meeting profoundly stirred up, feeling about as unspiritual as is possible. You may say things that you regret, or worse, say things that you do not know enough to regret until years later. And, the way places like AA work, you will not likely get kicked out. You will finish your rant and people will smile and say, "Keep coming back." Practicing stillness in the midst of strong inclinations to react, debate, and evaluate will serve you many places in life. And, while providing the other guy with a tolerant and patient environment, you may be paying rent for the day when it is you that needs the tolerance and patience. This is not to say you should seek this out. We encourage you to find meetings where there are a good number of people who speak in ways that are directly helpful. And, no matter how beloved the meeting, you will hear things that will give you a chance to practice stillness.

3

WILL YOU?

Growing Your Perspective Muscle

In the last chapter, we were exploring the cultivation of stillness, learning to notice the ways we lose the moment, and allowing ourselves, as a sort of meditation, to gently touch any costs of that loss over time. The end result of those exercises is to grow your stillness muscle. While we were doing that, we had also begun practicing taking a different point of view, a different perspective. In this chapter, we are going to learn about growing your perspective muscle even more. In order to do this, we will spend some time working on issues of *self*. We all use the word a lot in everyday conversation, and we mean a lot of different things when we do. We have a particular understanding of the word when we use it in this book, and it's worthwhile to talk about it some.

A very common use of the term in recent years is in the phrase "self-esteem." The basic idea is that if we feel bad about ourselves, we do badly, and therefore if we can make ourselves feel better, we will do better. It is a nice idea. But, in fact, lots of things make us *feel* better that do not make us *do* better. Drugs and alcohol are some very powerful feel-good technology, and if they made us do better, we wouldn't be writing this book and you wouldn't be reading it. It turns out that science has shown that the "feel good then do well idea" has some big problems.

The Self-Esteem Myth

One of the types of "view" our society has gotten very stuck on is the view we take of ourselves. We have been living for a good long time inside what psychologist Roy Baumeister calls the self-esteem myth (Baumeister, Campbell, Krueger, and Vohs 2005). The myth says that low self-esteem lies at the core of many individual and societal problems. We have been told that teen pregnancy, violence, school failure, and yes, even addiction, are the result of not thinking highly enough of ourselves. The self-esteem myth has been around for quite some time and has some powerful people and groups behind it. Baumeister and his colleagues point out that the state of California, in the late 1980s, even set up a governmental task force charged with raising the self-esteem of the state's young people. As the self-esteem myth gained momentum, it led to the development of the self-esteem industry. If you go into your local bookstore, you'll see that the shelves are filled with books that promise to show you how to improve your self-esteem. A search of a major online bookseller's site turns up more than 17,000 book titles linked to self-esteem.

Part of the myth tells us that we need to do something in order to raise our self-esteem. The myth tells us to seek self-esteem for ourselves and to promote it in our children. Every school-teacher has had it drummed into his or her head that he or she needs to make children have positive thoughts about themselves. Maybe you have even bought into the story that your difficulties are rooted in low self-esteem. But is it true?

During the last ten years, there has been a major effort by scientists to examine whether this story about the role of self-esteem is true. As it turns out, the answer is no. Although high self-esteem is sometimes related to positive things, it is also often related to surprisingly negative things. For example, high self-esteem is related to aggressiveness, bullying, narcissism, egotism, prejudice, and high-risk behaviors.

The Positive Affirmation Trap

A very popular strategy touted in the self-help books is the use of positive self-affirmations. Several studies have shown that getting people to say positive things about themselves seems to backfire for individuals who feel bad about themselves. For example, Joanne Wood and her colleagues placed students with high or low self-esteem in one of two situations. In one situation, students repeated positive self-statements such as, "I am a lovable person." In the other, students didn't repeat any statements. For individuals with high self-esteem, those who repeated positive statements showed very small positive changes in mood and incentive to engage in pleasant activities compared to those who did not repeat statements. For individuals with low self-esteem, those who repeated positive statements actually felt worse and reported a lower incentive to engage in pleasant activity than those who were not asked to repeat positive statements (Wood, Perunovic, and Lee 2009).

Even if there might be some reason to think that the occasional pep talk you might give yourself in the mirror isn't the worst thing in the world, the research evidence seems to point to the fact that deliberate attempts to raise your self-esteem are not necessarily going to result in feeling better about yourself or doing things in your life that you'll be happy about later. Even where there are positive effects, there is no good evidence that these pep talks have a lasting influence. This is not to say that we should not give encouragement for positive behavior we see in our children or spend our time with people who encourage us. It is simply to say that chasing the idea that you should "feel good about yourself" is not the path to a valued life.

You and Self-Esteem

Do some people drink or use drugs because they have low self-esteem? Maybe. But in those cases where substance abuse and low self-esteem might be tied together, it's often not clear which came first, the low self-esteem or the drinking or drug use. Do you drink because you don't value yourself highly, or do you not value yourself highly because you drink? For example, drug use can lead to poor performance at school and work. This poor performance can in turn lead to low self-esteem.

This same chicken-and-egg situation can be found in cases of high self-esteem also. High self-esteem is sometimes found to be connected to things like good grades and successful job performance, yet it could easily be the case that high performance actually causes the high self-esteem, not the other way around. Think about it this way: high levels of hot dog eating go with baseball game attendance. But increasing the number of hot dogs someone eats does not make it more likely that he or she will go to a ball game.

If it doesn't necessarily lead to good or bad things in your life, what's the deal with self-esteem? We think it comes down to this: self-esteem is a thought or collection of thoughts that you have. No more and no less. We all have thoughts all the time. Churning out thoughts is pretty much all our minds do all day long. Some of them don't get in your way as you go about living your life: *Look. A redwood tree.* Some, though, cause no end of trouble: *I really, really need a drink.* As far as we can tell, thoughts are thoughts, regardless of whether we think (still more thoughts) of them as good or bad. If working to change your thoughts related to self-esteem from negative to positive doesn't give good results, then you need to move on to something else.

Your Flexible Self

So, what does all of this mean? Well, we might have taken a slightly roundabout way to get there, but we're getting ready to introduce you to one of the more challenging aspects of ACT. To put it very bluntly (and maybe too simply, but we'll deal with that as we go along), the purpose of ACT *is not* to make you feel better about yourself, it's not to make you think more highly of yourself, and it's not even to get you to quit drinking or using drugs, necessarily. Instead, the goal of ACT is to develop something we and the other folks in the ACT community call *psychological flexibility.* This is a fancy phrase that basically means the ability to do whatever you choose to do, whenever you choose to do it, without being limited in your choices by what's going on inside your head.

You know what it means to be physically flexible, right? If we asked you to twist yourself up into a very advanced yoga position, your ability to do it would be limited by how physically flexible you are. If you're double-jointed and very limber, you'd roll yourself up on cue, slipping your feet behind your ears as easy as you please. But if you're like most of us, you're not a born contortionist. "My legs just won't go that way!" you might shout. You can sit Indian-style, but the lotus position is simply not something you can do. With time and diligent practice, you could probably condition yourself to do it. For now, though, you don't have the flexibility.

Psychological flexibility is pretty much the same thing. Let's say that instead of asking you to get into the lotus position, we asked you to give a speech to a large group of people. You might be a natural public speaker, and if you are, then you'd prepare your speech and step up to the microphone. As you know, though, public speaking is hard for lots of people. For many of us, even the mention of giving a speech will open the floodgates of the mind to a rush of paralyzing thoughts and feelings: *I'll make an ass of myself! Everyone will think I'm a total fool! Get me out of here!* There's nothing unusual about these kinds of reactions, and, frankly, it's why there aren't that many gifted public speakers. And if there's no particular reason for you to give a speech, then it's really not going to bother you all that much that you can't do it.

But what if your job required you to present ideas to a group? Or what if you felt strongly about an issue that was being discussed at a town meeting or your kid's PTA? What if you wanted to get up at an AA meeting and tell your story? If any of these things were important to you, your paralyzing thoughts and feelings would do a lot to limit what you can and can't do in your life. The same way you might not have the physical flexibility to get into the lotus position, you might not have the psychological flexibility to stand up in front of the PTA or the group at your AA meeting and speak out loud.

So the goal of ACT is to help you learn ways to build the psychological flexibility you need to do what you want, when you want, in your everyday life. If you've tried to get sober before, what happened the last time you wanted not to take a drink yet took it anyway? What raced through your head? What did you feel in your body? You might not remember, and you might not even have noticed at the time. This is one of the reasons we started our discussion with finding stillness in the present moment. If you practice going slowly when you want to, you'll have a better chance of catching those rushing thoughts and feelings in flight. *It'll just be this one drink, and I'll stop. I had a terrible fight with my wife, and I really need this one to take the edge off. I feel so alone. I don't want to hurt anymore.* Make no mistake: these thoughts are painful and scary. It's very natural for you to want to run from them. You may have been running from them for a long time. If you can find stillness, though, you might be able to recognize these thoughts as thoughts—and then choose to do what you planned to do all along, which is to not drink.

Flexibility in Finding Alternate Perspectives

The goal of ACT is psychological flexibility, so you've probably already guessed that everything you've read so far and will read from now on is all intended to help you limber up, psychologically speaking. This chapter on what it means to have a "self" is no exception.

Consider a case in which ACT treatment was given to people in a residential treatment program. One group had an ACT experience added to their regular drug and alcohol treatment and the other group just got the standard drug and alcohol treatment. At the end of the month in treatment, people who did not get the additional ACT treatment actually felt better about themselves than the people who got the usual drug and alcohol treatment. The people who got the ACT treatment reported lower self-esteem scores on a measure of shame than the group who got the usual treatment. This was just at the conclusion of the treatment, though. Three months later, when the psychologists checked in with the group members again, the situation had reversed itself. The people who got the ACT treatment, who felt worse when the treatment was over, actually reported feeling better about themselves three months later. And this effect continued for as long as the researchers followed the members of the group. In addition to feeling better about themselves, the people who received ACT treatment had fewer relapses over time. The other treatment made the people who got it feel better in the short term, but they felt worse and used more drugs and alcohol over the long term.

If the people in that study didn't chase momentary happiness, what did they do? They did a variety of things we will lead you through in this book, but one thing they did was to work on building flexibility in perspective taking—that is, they learned to look at and listen to themselves and the world around them in a variety of different ways, from different points of view.

Everybody likes an optimist, right? We might praise someone by remarking, "She's always so focused on the positives in life." Certainly, if you're always the doomsayer, you're not going to be very popular at dinner parties. It's natural (and, more importantly, comfortable) for people to try to focus on what, from their perspective, is "good." If you are in treatment, the positive view would be that treatment will be successful and that the path forward is a straight line to a good outcome. One characteristic of the non-ACT treatment in the study we mentioned earlier is that it was largely focused on the means the people in treatment could use to stop drinking and stay sober—that is, the means to a positive outcome after treatment. If you get too locked onto that positive view, though, you begin to screen out things that don't fit with that view. Problems get overlooked. Thoughts and emotions that go with problems get suppressed. What if you do want to drink? What kinds of feelings and experiences do you often associate with drinking? What kinds of costs have you paid as a result of drinking in the past? Talking about these kinds of things is not likely to leave you feeling great about yourself at the end of your treatment session. But *not talking* about them in treatment doesn't mean you won't be *having* them in the, oh, say, three months after treatment ends. Do the ACT vs. usual treatment results make a little more sense now? Long story short: there is a good deal of research that tells us, pretty clearly, that suppressing thoughts and emotions as a strategy is unworkable over the long term.

Another thing that can happen when people lock onto a particularly rosy view of the future is that they find that it is unsustainable, so they lurch between a rosy glow and gloom and doom overattachment to a negative perspective. *This is the same as every other time I tried to quit, and I know I am just going to blow it again!* The last chapter was about stillness. In this chapter we want to bring stillness together with flexible perspective taking.

Building Flexibility

You need to ask yourself this question: *Am I going to trade a moment's good feelings for living well?* This work, like in the story of the tortoise and the hare, is really more about slow and steady wins the race. If you are looking for a quick fix, this is not the place. If you worked on some of the inventories in the last chapter, you may understand why this is a slow and steady work and one that may cause some growing pains along the way. In this chapter, we will look back at some of the inventories we did in the last chapter and practice taking different perspectives on what was written.

Really showing up in your life—slowing down and meditating on exactly where you have come to in your life—can be painful. (There is an important distinction here between "meditate" and "ruminate." Meditation is about observing and noticing; rumination is about explaining and judging. Understand that the two are not interchangeable.) But not all pain is bad. Stubbing your toe is painful and damaging. Going to the gym can mean a certain amount of muscle pain, but it's not destructive pain. The work we are doing in this book is more like going to the gym. Over the short run, it can cause some pain. Over the long run, it can produce some real results. You can learn to tell the difference between destructive pain and healthy growing pains.

Based on the evidence, we do not advise you to chase self-esteem. Some people might suppose that there is some "just right" amount of self-esteem and then go about chasing the "just right" amount. We counsel against this for two reasons. First, no one has even demonstrated that there *is* such a magical level of self-esteem. And, second, getting into the business of managing your thoughts or feelings (including self-esteem) so that you can live more effectively is a little like managing clouds. There may be some number of clouds that is optimal for living, but clouds are notoriously hard to manage. And, while we have our hands and eyes pointed up toward these unruly, puffy clouds, we trip over obstacles that could be avoided and miss small things we could love that lie right there at our feet. ACT is like working when there are clouds *and* when there are no clouds…including the clouds that say, "I don't like it when it is this cloudy!"

Our work on self is not about winning the war about whether you are a good or bad person. It is more about ceasing to fight that battle. We will talk more about stepping out of the battle in the next two chapters on acceptance and holding stories lightly. Some of us have tried to win that fight and found the wins to be few and short-lived. Instead, we are going to grow our perspective muscle and perhaps see that there is a way forward that does not involve fighting—or at least we will be fighting fights that we have a shot at winning.

What Is a Perspective Muscle?

If you look at something from only one angle, you can know only a little bit about it. Look at the object below.

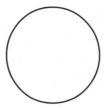

What is it? At first glance, you might be inclined to say a circle. But if you could look at it from a lot of different angles, you might find that it's not a two-dimensional circle. It could also be part of a cone or a funnel or a cylinder, or even the end of a long piece of plastic tubing. The only way to know it thoroughly would be to look at it from many points of view. In fact, if you could look very closely at the circle, you might see a very tiny wall of black ink (if you're reading this on paper) or an organized row of glowing pixels (if you're reading this on a screen.)

Perspective is a big deal. You can probably see examples of it in your own life. Have you ever seen two people in conflict? From outside of the conflict, you can sometimes see things that the people who are in conflict do not see. For example, sometimes in a divorce, the couple becomes so involved in fighting over who is right and who is wrong that they cannot see the harm that is being caused to the children. This is sometimes true even when both parents love the children.

Having your vision narrowly fixed means that you see some things very, very clearly, but it sometimes also means that there are a lot of things you miss. The trouble is that each member of the couple can see only from their own point of view. Imagine if they could see from their own perspective and the perspective of their spouse, perhaps not agreeing with the spouse, but allowing themselves to see the world from that place. Imagine they could see from the eyes of their own children. Imagine that both parents could close their eyes for a moment and picture their own child—seeing into the eyes of that child, perhaps seeing the fear in that small face. Imagine that they could pour their awareness into the child's body and open their eyes, seeing from the eyes of the child. Picture how terrifying the world looks from that child's eyes—two beloved people, deep in battle. Imagine if the parents could come to stillness in that witnessed moment. Such flexibility in perspective causes the world to look a little different. Our view is richer. Being able to see a bit from all these perspectives makes it less likely people will miss things they care about.

There is an ancient story from India that tells of six blind men who were to determine what an elephant looked like by feeling it. The one who felt the trunk said it was like a water spout.

The one who felt the leg said it was like a pillar. The one who felt the side said it was like a wall. The one that felt the tusk said it was like a pipe. The one who felt the tail said an elephant is like a rope. Imagine that "what an elephant is like" was a good reason to go to war! They could all get their armies together and battle it out. Losses would mount. In the end someone would win, but many more would lose. The irony is that they were all correct, but only from a limited perspective. Again, look at the advantage offered by multiple perspectives.

Hitting the Road

I have a personal example of this. Teenagers often feel misunderstood by adults in their lives. I left home when I was sixteen years old. This was most definitely a bad idea. My home life was fine. I had a great mom and a stepfather who loved me without limit. But the late sixties and early seventies were tumultuous times. I dropped out of high school and had no permanent address. There was a whole generation of us hitchhiking around the country, riding our thumbs to wherever they might take us.

I recall one particular trip. I had stopped in to see my mom and dad in Spokane, Washington. After a couple of days at their place, I had my mom drop my friend Shawn and me off on Highway 395 so we could hitch up to Canada, just to look around. We had our backpacks, our sleeping bags, and five dollars between us. As a parent, in this moment, I feel like I should call my mom and tell her how sorry I am to have put her through that. I am sure she went home and cried her eyes out.

Could I see it? Nope, not one bit. We just saw ourselves as free spirits, unencumbered by material possessions. In a certain sense we were right about that, but we failed to see a lot that was wrong in our behavior. I lived very carelessly like that for a long time and was fortunate enough to live to tell about it. But a good number of my buddies from those careless days found their way to the graveyard.

Part of what we call wisdom and maturity has to do with being able to see from different perspectives. Mature does not mean "over twenty-one years of age" and wise does not mean "knows a lot of facts." Lots of people are over twenty-one and are not mature. Lots of people know a lot of facts but are not wise. I did not even really start to grow up until I was thirty. It was at the age of thirty in 1985 that I started to look back. I started to look ahead. I started to look at my lot in life from the view of my ten-year-old daughter, her mother, my wife, my parents, the community. I started to look ahead as well as backward. I started listening to people who saw in me things that I could not see in myself. This last was perhaps the hardest—trying to see with the eyes of people who saw possibility in me. I stopped seeing the world through a single lens and things started to look different. Let me be clear: I am not saying that I am wise or mature, but I feel like I'm on track, and I endeavor to practice the things spoken of in this book persistently.

Working It Out

It's kind of hard to know where and when you'll want or need to look at your life from a different perspective. It's like someone once said about art: you'll know what the uses are when you see 'em.

The two little exercises that follow are good for learning what it feels like to drop in and out of alternate perspectives. As with the stillness exercises in the last section, please approach each one of these gently. Skillful perspective taking takes time to develop, and there is no guarantee that what you'll see with your fresh eyes will be easy or pleasant over the short term. It does make it more likely that you'll like what you see over the long term, though. Be kind to yourself as you go.

◀ The "Who Am I?" Exercise

In this little exercise, we will explore the question "Who am I?" We don't mean this in any goofy sense. We mean it in a very simple sense. People confuse who they are with what they see when they look at different bits of their experience. And this can lead to a lot of problems. Sometimes people confuse themselves with their job. If you think that your job defines you, and your job goes away, it can be like dying. Sometimes people confuse themselves with their body. If you have a model's body or a super athletic body, and anything happens, like age or disability, it is like losing "you." This is a pretty easy mistake to see when it is happening to someone else, but not so easy to detect when it is happening to you. There are a thousand stories we tell about ourselves that define us. The problem is that the stories can become traps and we end up living inside the trap. If we hold rigidly to a story about being a "good person," we sometimes blind ourselves to places we are going wrong. If we hold rigidly to a story about how bad we are, we sometimes miss what we are doing right in our lives.

Am I my body? If someone walks into a room and says, "Where is Kelly Wilson?" I might point toward my own chest and say: "Right here." Everywhere I have ever gone, my body was there. But am I my body?

Think of a time when you were little—maybe six or seven. If you have a picture, take a look. Describe that small child's body in just a sentence or two. See if you can close your eyes and picture yourself in that body.

Posed, earnest. Put together, cared for. Posed & self-aware, perhaps (at Grandparents house) overly self-conscious. Anticipating, but appearing comfortable/content.

Think of a time when you were a teenager. See yourself then. Close your eyes and see if you can remember what it was like being in that body.

I remember feeling restless - ready to grow up. I was self-critical, but prideful about my body at the same time.

Describe a particular time when your body was at its healthiest. Close your eyes and see if you can recall what that was like.

23 - kickboxing regularly. I felt strong. I felt confident in how I looked and what I could do. Working early hours & making regular workouts.

Describe a particular time when you were very, very sick.

LA - 31. I had a sore throat/cough for a month (plus). I developed vertigo, lost my balance, & fell over. Made plans to move back East that day.

Now let's look at emotion. Think of a time when you were very sad. Picture yourself in that moment. See if you can picture your own face. See if you can see the sadness in those eyes, in the way that you hold your body. Describe what you see.

Grief stricken. 4 months after my Dad passed. Visiting LA for the first time. I was shaken, over weight, hair too blonde, I felt lost, without a compass.

Now think of a time when you were truly happy. See if you can picture or even feel the way you held your face, the way you moved, the way you sounded when you laughed. Describe what you see.

Seeing Nikki on our apartment floor after getting her from the shelter. She was recovering from her surgery. I was so happy she was my (+ AJ's) very own dog. I was 20. Just off work — giddy, excited, joyful. Spoke to her like a baby.

Now let's look at thoughts. See if you can think of a belief you had when you were little that you no longer believe. Maybe you believed in Santa Claus? Write that down.

All dogs were boys and all cats were girls. Also, did not understand the intimacy of the sexual act.

What are some really serious thoughts you have had? Maybe about your health? Or finances? Let your eyes go closed for a moment and see if you can picture yourself in the middle of those thoughts. Write a few down.

If I continue to drink excessively I'll get breast cancer. That everyone dear to me will die + I'll be alone.

Think now about roles you have had in your life. When have you been a child, a student, a team member, a bully, a victim? What about a parent, a teacher, a coach, a spouse, someone who was left or who did the leaving in a relationship?

> Child. Confidant. Nominee (Student council)
> Victim. Student. Actress. Other woman. Singer.
> (mother) Cheerleader.
> Damsel. Girlfriend. Drop out (college) Employee.
> Friend. Did the leaving (2x) Was left. (1x) Dancer.

Now, get a mirror and take a look into your own eyes, and see if you can see the you in there that looked out of the eyes of that child, that teenager, that sick body, that healthy body. See if you can let it sink in that there is a you that has been there the whole time.

> I wonder where I was before and why we cannot remember. Perhaps it's best to only have one journey at a time.

Who was it that noticed all those bodies, emotions, roles, thoughts?

> My higher self. My soul. The "me" that's always existed above the physical me + observed my thoughts + actions.

◀ ## AN ANSWER FROM THE ME I WOULD BE: A LETTER TO THE PAST

For this exercise, get a pen and paper. It might help if you can find a picture of yourself when you were a child. If not, then just close your eyes and imagine your own face as a child.

Begin the exercise by imagining, even if it does not seem to be true right now, that you are right on track in your life in this moment. Not that everything is great right now, but that you are on the road to a life you could really love. If you are very off track right now, you notice that it is possible that today is a crossroads and that looking back later in your life, you would look at today and say, "That was the day things began to shift. I could not even see it then. Things looked hopeless, but I was wrong. And I can see now that that was the day I put my feet on the ground and began my journey to a better life."

Close your eyes for a moment and allow yourself to imagine that it is so. We don't mean this as some sort of self-esteem builder. We covered that ground earlier in the chapter. We also don't mean it as a promise. None of us can know the future. Just imagine that it is so. Let it be possible, even though your mind may say, *Impossible!* Just allow your eyes to go closed. Picture your self on this day, and let it be so, in your imagination, that this day was *the* day, the turning point. If your mind gets busy in this imagining, just practice Six Breaths on Purpose and let the thoughts bubble. You don't need to drive them away. Really try to see your own face in your mind's eye and let yourself see in that face someone who is on the path. Take a couple of minutes.

On a sheet of paper, jot down a few notes about what your mind had to tell you during that little meditation. These will be just for your reference after you complete the rest of the exercise. After you have written down what you need to, turn your paper over.

If you have a photo of yourself as a youngster, set it in front of you. Look into your own eyes and come to stillness. If you don't have a photo, allow your mind to reach back to a moment from your childhood that you remember clearly. See yourself in that moment: what you looked like, what you were wearing, and your surroundings. Sit for as long as you like while you breathe in and out this image of yourself as a youngster.

When you're ready, take up your pen and paper, and write a short letter to yourself as a young child, from the perspective you imagined above, where today would be the day you turned everything around. What will that young person need to go through to get where you are today? Don't try to rewrite history. You've suffered, and that young person will suffer too. You know that he or she will suffer, and there's nothing you can do to prevent that. But if today were the day that your life turned around, what message would you have to offer your young self? What gift could you give? What about that young person's experience have you come to treasure now, even if it was impossibly hard at the time? Breathe. Take your time. If hard things come up, let them. Don't push them away. Just go quiet. And when you're ready, continue.

When you're finished, put down your pen and paper. Let your eyes go closed and take a few long, deep breaths before you set down this piece of work. Maybe go get some air before coming back to your letter. Try reading it aloud. Make a few notes about what kinds of things this exercise brought into—or caused to spill out of—your inclined heart.

◄

Yet Another Perspective: Acceptance

We hope you've made a little mental note to keep trying to understand—feel, really—how these ideas we're discussing with you fit into the bigger idea of psychological flexibility. We're looking to find an answer to the question "How can I find a way to do what I choose to do in my life, even when I'm hurting, even when I doubt that I can make the choices I want to make?" Being still when it matters is one way. Seeing things from perspectives other than your most instinctive or most practiced is another. Now we'll move on to another aspect of flexibility. It's about finding a way to be all right with the fact that your life, all of our lives, are filled with experiences that are sweet or sad, and sometimes both at once. In a word, we call this way *acceptance*.

AA AND THE GIFT OF PERSPECTIVE

Although the 12-step literature does not contain a lot of direct talk about perspective taking, the steps contain many opportunities. Individuals who have been treated from a 12-step perspective are often asked to do a substance use history, perhaps not unlike the substance use history we asked for in the last chapter. Making an inventory of using and its costs, and putting it all down in black and white, can sometimes cause it to come into view in a different way. Rumbling around in our heads, these things can drain the life from us. Sometimes the simple putting of pen to paper can allow you to see your own flaws with enough distance to encounter yourself with kindness and humility.

Humility is mentioned often in 12-step programs. It is an interesting concept. It does not mean humiliation. One cool way to think of humility is offered by historian John Dickson. Humility, says Dickson, is the dignified choice to willingly forgo status and offer resources for the good of others (this is in Dickson's book *Humilitas*, published in 2011). Dickson identifies three key elements in this definition. First, the definition assumes dignity. That is, it assumes that the person is in possession of some resource. If you have the strength to straighten chairs and serve coffee at a meeting, you have resources to offer. Second, humility is freely chosen. Humiliation is different. Humiliation is visited upon us. You do not have to serve, but the humble serve. And the final quality identified by Dickson is that humility is social—it is service to our fellows. Even believers in God, who see all service as ultimately to God, will find in their spiritual tradition a sense of the importance of offering yourself in service to your fellows. Such a perspective on humility will take you a long way in Alcoholics Anonymous.

Another major place where perspective taking is used again and again is in the fourth step: "We made a searching and fearless moral inventory of ourselves." The details of the fourth step are worth reviewing here. I have used this inventory with plenty of people, including many who had no drug or alcohol problem at all. Why? Because the inventory deals primarily with the problem of resentment, and although the AA Big Book suggests this is something peculiarly important for alcoholics, in my experience it is a big problem for a lot of people.

The fourth-step inventory begins with a list of resentments. Members are asked to look back over their lives and make a list of persons, institutions, and principles with whom they are angry. Sometimes just getting this list on paper can cause people to be a bit shocked at the breadth of their resentments. Next, beside each, they are asked to write what impact the resented party had. Did they threaten or damage a sense of self-worth, some ambition, financial security, or interpersonal relations? Next, members are asked to view these individuals as perhaps spiritually sick. "Though we did not like their symptoms and the ways they disturbed us, they, like ourselves were sick too" (AA, p. 67). Individuals are asked to go back to the list and attempt to view each person from this perspective and to pray for each in turn.

From an ACT view, it would be very helpful to painstakingly take the time for each person on the list, attempting to imagine the very real possibility that this person who had caused harm was operating out of past wrongs done them, out of vulnerability, or perhaps fear. Perhaps your bullying boss has a history of being bullied. Perhaps she feels terribly insecure and bullies and acts competent in order to hide that. You won't know whether any of this is true, but taking time to imagine how this might be so can change your viewpoint and, in doing so, exercise that perspective muscle you've been working on. This is not done in order to justify someone's bad behavior. Just because behavior is understandable does not make it good or acceptable. For example, in a war zone you might understand why the people on each side are shooting at one another. However, you would still not want to walk around on the battlefield. Bullets fired for good reasons or bad reasons are equally deadly. Nor is practice at perspective taking done in order to correct your wrong ideas or evaluations or to make you into a saint. It is simply the case that being able to see things from the other guy's perspective is an asset. The potential benefit to you lies in your increasing skill at taking different perspectives. If your car died and you had an idea about what was wrong, you might open the hood and take a look. Looking might change your mind and it might not. But the person who knows how to check under the hood is in better shape than someone who cannot. Taking other perspectives is a way you can check under the hood in your relations with others. And, as in the first and fourth steps, it's a way to check under the hood of your relationship with past and future versions of yourself.

Another place to practice perspective taking is in 12-step meetings. The way meetings typically proceed is that one person speaks at a time. We encourage you to let go of comparison and evaluation while listening. Try to see from the eyes and hear from the ears of others. This does not mean that you have to agree or follow any advice they might give. You will hear people in meetings who are incredibly trapped in their stories about themselves. And you will also hear stories of self-discovery, of people finding things within themselves that they never knew existed. You will surely hear stories of people who have lived long enough to transcend their own stories about themselves. See if it is possible to take a kindly and compassionate view of the ones who seem trapped. That someone might be you on a particularly difficult day. As you listen to those who have let go of old stories and who are actively curious about the ongoing story they are writing with their lives, pay special attention, and allow yourself to become curious about what your story might look like if you were to rise above it and chose a new and vital direction. You might ask one of these people if he or she would like to go to coffee afterward or which meetings he or she likes. Someone like that might be a good candidate as a 12-step sponsor. You might find that this person's perspective on other good meetings puts you into some very interesting meetings.

4

The Sweet and the Sad

The title of this book, as you'll recognize if you have any experience with AA (and probably regardless), is a part of the Serenity Prayer. Probably first written down in the 1930s and often credited to the the theologian Reinhold Niebuhr, the prayer has been expressed in a few different ways, one of which is now strongly associated with AA and other 12-step programs:

> God grant me the serenity to accept the things I cannot change,
> The courage to change the things I can,
> And the wisdom to know the difference.

Since we cribbed the title of this book from the prayer, you won't be very surprised to learn that we think a good deal of what we have to say in this book is expressed with uncommon simplicity and elegance in these three lines. Of the six pieces, or processes, we'll talk about in the book, the prayer directly addresses two: acceptance, which is the subject of this chapter, and commitment, which we'll get to in chapter 7.

Opening Up

You can start your adventures in acceptance right now, by letting go of any tension you feel about reading a "prayer" or seeing the mention of the word "God." We don't know you, reader, so we don't know how you feel about these words. For some people, these are extremely important words. For others, they are sources of discomfort. For now, though, set aside the idea that these three lines are a prayer and that they're directed at God. And set aside the fact that AA has adopted them and shared them with so many. Whatever your religious views or your opinion of AA, there is a lot that's useful to us in these three lines without taking those things into consideration.

The first line of the prayer asks for the serenity to accept things we cannot change. And while it seems almost too obvious to mention, there are actually a whole lot of things that we simply can't change about the world and ourselves. If your eyes are brown, they're brown. If you miss your train at the station, you miss your train. If you've been drinking for twenty years, you've been drinking for twenty years.

Sometimes the things we cannot change are more daunting than the color of our eyes or a missed train, though. Sometimes they are even more daunting than a long history of drinking problems. Austrian psychiatrist Viktor Frankl, in his book *Man's Search for Meaning* (1984), describes an experience he had while imprisoned in a Nazi concentration camp during World War II. He speaks at length about suffering in the camps, which is no surprise. However, the point upon which the entire book turns is Frankl's description of the time he and a companion find a way to escape the camp. They gather some food and a few other supplies. The day before their planned escape, Frankl decides to make one last round with the patients in his makeshift hospital. He knows that his attempts to care for his fellows are not going to save many of them. The prisoners under his care are sick and starving, and he has few resources with which to help them. In fact, he has little to offer them except comfort.

Frankl describes one fellow he had been particularly keen on saving, but who was clearly dying. On Frankl's last round, the man looks into his eyes and says, "You, too, are getting out?"

Frankl writes, "I decided to take fate into my own hands for once." (79) He tells his friend that he will stay in the camp and care for his patients. Upon returning to sit with his patients, Frankl describes a sense of peace unlike any he had ever experienced.

Faced with some of the cruelest circumstances ever devised, Frankl found freedom that day in the camp by accepting his circumstances and choosing a course that mattered to him. He chose to be "Viktor Frankl, the man who did what he could to care for his patients" rather than "Viktor Frankl, the man who escaped." We'll have more to say about the choice Frankl made when we discuss values a little later. For now, the thing to note is that, in order to make his choice, Frankl needed to accept some things that, for most of us, are only the stuff of nightmares, and he found incredible freedom in that act of acceptance.

What Acceptance Looks Like

We define acceptance as remaining intentionally open and receptive to whatever it is that you experience at any given time. Acceptance means being willing to feel what you feel, think what you think, and see and hear what you see and hear—even when what you feel, think, or perceive is unpleasant or painful.

Acceptance Isn't Approving, Wanting, or Liking

Do you remember the distinction we drew in the last chapter between meditation and rumination? When you meditate on something, you consider it, notice it, and observe it. When you ruminate on something, you judge it, evaluate it, or try to solve it. Taken this way, acceptance is like meditation in that it's necessarily free from judgments, evaluations, and desire. When you accept something, it doesn't mean that you're going to approve of it, like it, or want it. If you feel yourself come down with the flu, you can accept the thoughts that arise about getting sick, being uncomfortable, and so forth without wanting or liking the illness. Acceptance means that when a particular experience arises, you find a way to acknowledge it, be present to it, and take it in without attempts to alter it in any way.

This doesn't mean that judgments go away or need to go away, though. As you lie in bed with the flu, you're likely to be thinking about how lousy it is to be confined to bed with fever and chills. You might wish you didn't have the flu.

Two Paths to Letting Go

Acceptance and letting go of struggle have been enormously important in my own recovery. I think they can be in yours too. There are two paths I know of to letting go. One path to letting go involves holding onto something, anything, really tightly. If you are holding something tightly and are approached by a person carrying a baseball bat, and the person hits you with the bat repeatedly, you will eventually let go. This was my path to acceptance and letting go. I took a tremendous beating—physically, emotionally, psychologically, and financially, unto death really—before I let go. I do not recommend this path.

There is an easier way. Just let go. I doubt there is anyone reading this book who has not taken a beating. Maybe more than me, maybe less (I hope less). The good news is that you get to decide how much of a beating is necessary.

Acceptance Isn't Resignation

Another subtle distinction is between acceptance and resignation. Resignation involves some aspects that are similar to acceptance. For example, if you are resigned to something, you may no longer fight it. However, resignation often involves a sort of giving up on life and on possibilities. Acceptance in ACT is more like opening up than it is like giving up.

The Opposite of Acceptance

The opposite of acceptance, as we understand it, is called *avoidance*. It's probably easy for you to imagine what avoidance might look like. It's an unwillingness to be open to the things that make up acceptance.

Avoidance is something that you might want to spend some extra time thinking about because, from an ACT perspective, we can often describe drinking and drug use as kinds of avoidance behaviors. What kinds of things make you want to drink or use? Feeling tense in social situations? Being in physical pain? Feeling lonely? Angry? Hopeless? Or even uneasy and uncertain about whether you'll stay clean and sober? None of these experiences are going to feel very good. Actually, they're all going to hurt quite a lot. If you're not willing to have those experiences—if you're unable, in other words, to practice acceptance with respect to these experiences—you can attempt to avoid them by drinking or using.

It's a plain fact: it's raining someplace all the time. No one gets through life without getting hurt. Everyone and everything that matters to you will one day slip from your grasp and be lost to you forever. No one alive today is going to stay that way—at least not in his current form. Living hurts like hell, at least some of the time. Each time we turn away, slip around, or close up to painful experience, we run the very real risk of our world shrinking just a little bit. With a lifetime of avoidance like this, your world can become very small indeed.

How Much Pain Can you Stand?

People often think that there is a line across the universe of pain. On one side of the line is the amount of pain a person can stand. On the other side of that line lies "too much." The truth, I think, is that we do not know how much pain a human can stand. History is filled with people who have suffered extraordinary pain in the service of something they valued. For example, in probably every war in history, there have been people in the middle of a war zone who handed their children to a stranger on the back of a cart or a truck, knowing that they would never see them again. They did so because they knew that to keep them meant condemning them to death. Like Frankl's decision to remain in the camp to care for his probably hopeless patients, these are acts of heroism.

A Call to Your Own Personal Heroism

What if you could be a hero? Since I cleaned up in 1985, I have seen heroism and sought stories of it. These stories have been like food for me over the years. I have listened for them and tried to hear the heart of them. I have read stories of Martin Luther King's civil rights heroism and Gandhi's country-freeing heroism and Mandela's apartheid-ending heroism. I have also listened to small stories of heroism. President Barack Obama tells of his mother getting up before dawn each morning to tutor him before he went off to school and she went off to work. This sounds like heroism to me.

I have been looking for the common thread that connects these stories, and I think I have found it. The common thread is that these acts all involve people doing the next right thing in their own lives. What they did day-by-day was hard and it was for a purpose. Gandhi's great fasts involved going the next hour without food, and the next. Mandela's heroism involved bearing each day of hard labor in the lime quarry—this rock and the next, one after another. And King: this step, in this march, and the next. And President Obama's mother, rising at 4 a.m. to tutor a son, this morning, and the next. All these stories, large and small, involve pain and purpose.

As I read these stories I ask myself what this might look like this day in my own life. What is before me? Here is a story:

As a father of three children, my first reaction is to say that I cannot imagine the pain of letting a child go. My second reaction is to recall that cold fall morning in Seattle in 1978 when I let my oldest daughter slip away because I lived inside the story that I could not tolerate the pain of life without drugs and alcohol. Recent years suggest that that story, which seemed so completely and absolutely true at the time, was false. I have in fact lived smack in the middle of life without drugs and alcohol for more than twenty-five years. And I have walked through a fair bit of pain over those years—treatment for hepatitis C, cancer, the deaths of two of my brothers. (And I have also been deep into nonacceptance a lot of times. A lot.)

There aren't that many Gandhis and Mandelas and Kings. But there are many, many heroes: men and women who make the decision that one day will be their day to pick something different for their lives. You have that capacity for heroics inside of you, whether or not you believe it now.

Acceptance Isn't Good; Avoidance Isn't Bad

It's worth a mention here, all good notwithstanding, that acceptance isn't an end unto itself—nobody gets a medal or merit badge for being accepting—and, so far as we know, there are no avoidance police. If you need to get a root canal, we strongly recommend you accept when the dentist offers you the novocaine. Miring yourself in pain for its own sake isn't the idea here.

As with learning to be still and learning to see things from different perspectives, any efforts you make to be more accepting are in the service of developing greater psychological flexibility—the ability to do what you choose, when you choose, even if things are going on in your head or in your life that make it hard. When painful experience gets between you and what you want, acceptance is the skill you need to keep your feet moving through the hard stuff and keep heading in the direction you want to go. Avoidance, on the other hand, is what you might do—and might have done in the past—to get away from the painful experiences.

Still, it might be worth noting that there is an ever-growing body of research evidence that suggests attempts to suppress negative thoughts and emotions can have detrimental effects (Purdon 1999; Roemer and Borkovec 1994; Wegner et al. 1987). There's also evidence that suggests that openness and acceptance foster good long-term outcomes (Gifford et al. 2006; Hayes et al. 2006).

◀ THE COST OF AVOIDANCE

Let's take a little pause here to reflect on times in your life when you've been unwilling to have certain experiences. Before you start recording your answers, take a few moments to sit quietly with your eyes gently closed. Reflect on experiences you may have had in which there were thoughts, feelings, physical sensations, or a sense of uncertainty that you simply were unwilling to have. Don't rush into writing about this. Just call them to mind and wonder about them for a while. And breathe.

When you're ready, make notes about some of these experiences. What were they? What did you do to avoid them? How did this work out for you in the short term—say, the same day or within a few days? And how did your attempts to avoid the painful experience work out for you in the long term? You can use the table below or record your thoughts in a notebook.

Thought/situation I avoided	How I avoided it	What happened right then	What happened eventually
Taking class at Margie Haber	Forfeited my 1st month deposit, called	I was made to feel bad by the teacher	I moved on to study at Warner's
Pilates certification	Told them I couldn't commit to it	Lost my deposit ($150) (had more free time)	I started doing the Bar Method
Taking pills reco. to stop bleeding	Never ordered them.	Periods remained heavy.	My iron was low. Ordered the pills. (After 1 year).
Going into work when scheduled.	Called out.	Had to pick another night/ deal with uncertainty.	Un-resolved.
Responsibility/ Working a job - not having freedom.			

What do you take away from the notes you've made above? Do you see any kind of a pattern? And if you do, how does it compare with what we've suggested about acceptance and avoidance? Do you generally find that attempting to avoid negative experience has resulted in positive consequences? Or have you suffered as a result of avoidance?

Thoughts - 30 days is avg. my limit before I start to sabotage/leave. (lately) ◀

Control Freak

There's more to not being accepting than running and hiding or blotting out painful experiences with alcohol or drugs. Some of us try to mitigate painful emotions by clamping down, suppressing, or trying to micromanage our experiences.

Controlling and Supressing Emotions

You won't be terribly surprised to learn that attempts to control or suppress strong negative feelings and emotions don't work much better than avoiding them. Psychologist James Pennebaker pioneered a series of writing studies in which participants wrote about difficult situations. Most of the studies involved participants writing about a difficult topic for approximately twenty minutes on three separate days. In their writing instructions, they were encouraged to write about their deepest feelings regarding the difficult topic.

Pennebaker's results suggest that expressing these powerful feelings had some positive results (and recall that, in order to express them, you more or less need to accept them). A group of workers laid off from their jobs who wrote about the pain of being laid off were reemployed more rapidly than workers who didn't do this writing (Spera, Buhrfeind, and Pennebaker 1994). College freshmen who wrote about their difficulties in school showed fewer health care visits and better grades (Pennebaker and Beall 1986).

Now, just because there are some studies to suggest that expression of strong emotions is perhaps beneficial at times, don't imagine that we're saying it's healthy to just go around expressing yourself everywhere you go. That's not the message. Some people just don't want to hear it. If they're in a position to do you harm, they might. Remember that the people in the Pennebaker studies usually do their expressing in complete privacy. Also, the habit of keeping emotions to ourselves in an effort to control them often gets extended from places where it is necessary to places where it is not necessary. For example, there are a lot of things that might be a problem if they were expressed at work that can be freely shared in an AA meeting.

◄ The Cost of Emotional Control

Let's do a little inventory, similar to the one that you did before for situations and experiences you might have avoided. This time, though, let's think about situations when you've tried to suppress or control emotions or feelings you may have had. Once again, you can work on the page below or in a notebook, but before you put pen to paper, take at least a few long, deep breaths and really allow your memories of these experiences to rise up inside you. Sit with them for a while and, when you're ready, make your notes.

Thought/situation I controlled	How I controlled it	What happened right then	What happened eventually

Just as you did before, take a little time to look over your notes. Wonder a little about the patterns you're observing. In general, do you think your attempts at controlling or suppressing painful emotions have been helpful, harmful, or neutral in your life?

◄

Controlling Physical Sensations

The story is pretty much the same in the world of physical sensations as it is for emotions. Acceptance of them makes them easier to live with and results in better outcomes than avoiding them or trying to control them. This similarity makes a good deal of sense, since your brain and your body are all part of the same you. What you feel in your body is very likely to stir up your thoughts, and vice versa.

Consider people diagnosed with panic disorder. They experience panic attacks—periods of anxiety so extreme that they feel as if they are going to go crazy or die. People who have panic attacks sometimes begin to avoid any situation where they fear they might have a panic attack.

So, for example, they might not go to the store during a busy time because they fear they might have a panic attack while in line and not be able to readily get out of the store. But another thing that people with panic often do is to avoid bodily sensations that are connected to anxiety. So, for example, they might stop exercising because it makes their heart rate go up—just like it does when they have a panic attack. But it turns out that the more people avoid places (like the store) or sensations (like a racing heart), the more disabled they become.

Another area that is relevant to physical sensations is chronic pain. It works in very much the same way as with panic. People experiencing chronic pain begin to bend their lives in ways that help them avoid pain—at least in the short run. The problem is that the ways they avoid pain in the short run—by staying in bed, using narcotic pain medications, reducing activity, for example—can backfire in the long run. The more you avoid the pain sensations, the more disabled you become. The longer you lie down, the less likely it is that you will ever get up. Lying down, getting small, reducing activity, all work over the short terms but are disabling over the long term. The strategies are a trap.

There can be a lot of physical sensations that are connected to letting go of substances. Sometimes it is the physical discomfort of detox. Don't underestimate this. Some people who are extremely physically dependent on drugs such as alcohol can have life-threatening physical withdrawal symptoms. But even relatively small regular amounts of drug and alcohol intake can result in non–life-threatening, yet uncomfortable, physical symptoms when those intakes are removed. For example, it is common to experience vague physical discomfort while in situations that are connected strongly to drinking or using. Sometimes we just feel out of place, like our skin does not quite fit. And, running in the back of the mind is the certainty of how immediately a drink or hit would dissolve that discomfort. But like pain and panic and a hundred other physical sensations, the short-term benefit of retreat ends up being buried by the cost of the retreat.

The best medicine for this is to grow your acceptance muscle. As we described above, acceptance does not mean brutally forcing yourself into different situations or gritting your teeth. It means taking yourself to hard experiences with kindness and compassion. It means noticing the ways we tense up and say "no" with our body, mind, and behavior.

◀ CHECKING IN WITH YOUR BODY

This is a simple meditation of the body-scan variety common to a range of mindfulness-oriented practices. The idea is to become aware of sensations in your body, deliberately and gradually—to just notice them and let them be, without evaluating or controlling them. Honestly, you'll benefit the most from this kind of practice if you're not in severe pain or experiencing detox symptoms at the moment. It will be a lot easier to relax, notice, and accept physical sensations in your body if they're not causing you extraordinary discomfort. Practicing this kind of awareness exercise is cumulative: the more you do it, the more natural it will seem, even if you are in pain. But we need to meet life where we are, not where we'd ideally prefer to be. So, if you are in pain or withdrawal, you can still try this exercise. Be especially kind and compassionate to yourself, though, if you find your attention falling apart or your patience wearing thin.

1. Start by loosening your collar and belt. Kick off your shoes, and find a comfortable place where you can lie down with your arms at your side. If it's more comfortable for you, you can place a pillow under your head and another behind your knees.

2. Take four long, slow deep breaths, allowing the air to fill up your belly first and then your chest. Exhale slowly. Once you've finished, just allow your breath to flow naturally for the rest of the exercise, without trying to slow it down or make it deeper intentionally.

3. Start first by letting your attention flow into the soles of your feet. See if there is any sensation there, any tension or pain. Can you feel the weight of your socks? The floor beneath your heels?

4. Gradually allow your awareness to travel from your feet into your legs, through your belly and chest, down your arms, and back up, until you come to the top of your head. *Take your time with this.* Pay attention to everything you notice: warmth or coolness; the feel of fabric on your hair; the motion of air across your skin if you're in a draft.

5. When you've completely scanned your entire body, call to mind any place where you're feeling pain or tension. If your head hurts, for example, allow your awareness to flow into the pain. What does it feel like? Sharp? Stabbing? Dull? Does it change when your heart beats? What about when you breathe in or out?

6. While you keep your attention focused on the painful sensation, take one of your hands from your side and place it over the place where it hurts. Does the warmth of your hand change the sensation? See if you can find a way to relate to the pain that doesn't seek to get rid of it or evaluate it. See if you can find a way to appreciate the way it changes from moment to moment. Try to imagine, even for a moment, what it would be like to make a place for this pain in your life, to welcome it as part of who you are. Yes, this will be a frightening thing to think about, especially if you're in a lot of discomfort. But try to see how this change in relationship affects your experience of the pain itself.

The goal of this exercise is to help you learn how it feels to simply be aware of painful sensations, to perhaps get a sense about ways in which you can act in your life even with pain present.

◀

Reflecting on the Sweet and the Sad

What's really at the bottom of this acceptance/avoidance problem? Simply this: sweetness and sadness very often, if not always, live in the same house. Think about it for a moment. If you cared about nothing, nothing could cause you pain. You need to care in order to feel pain.

We want to close this chapter with an exercise that has come to mean a lot to both of us. It's called the Sweet Spot. It's a little meditation you can do with a partner about a moment when you knew sweetness in your life. Both you and your partner will have a sweet moment in mind when you begin. After spending some time reflecting on your moment of sweetness, each of you will take turns expressing about your moment of sweetness to the other. The job of the expresser is to just express—not to explain, justify, or make any sense. The job of the listener is merely to appreciate—not to sympathize, encourage, or reinforce. Get it? Just noticing, accepting, not judging.

The funny thing about Sweet Spot is that, when people do it, they very often end up crying. Nothing about this should come as a surprise. Same house, remember? We could have just as easily called it the Sad Spot, because our moments of greatest sweetness are very often etched through with things that are terribly sad. And what's the moral of this story? If you don't open your heart up to sadness, you're likely to cut yourself off from sweetness at the same time.

(A word of caution: the directions we give for the Sweet Spot below are, frankly, too short. It's a meditation on a moment, and it's something that, if you were sitting in the room with Kelly, would feel dramatically different than it will if you read the directions and follow along. So, we're splitting the difference: the directions below are an edited transcript of an exercise like this that Kelly has led in the past. You can get the idea of Sweet Spot by reading them, and you may have a good experience by just approximating them with your partner by taking turns. If you can, though, you should download the audio record of Kelly leading Sweet Spot that we've made available at nhpubs.com/9288. It's there in MP3 audio that you can easily add to your portable music player or listen to right in your web browser. He walks you through the whole exercise during the course of the recording. This is really how we recommend experiencing the Sweet Spot.)

◄ Sweet Spot

Get yourself a notebook and a pencil or a pen. Allow yourself to sit comfortably—maybe with your feet on the ground. Just gently, gently let your eyes close.

I'd like you to begin by noticing the different sounds in the room. Imagine that you have a sort of checklist. Begin with the most prominent sounds, and just as you notice them, imagine that you check them off the list. See if you can listen for smaller, more subtle sounds. You might hear the sounds of vehicles outside or the sound of a jackhammer way off in the distance. If you listen carefully, you might hear the sounds of people around you. Breathe.

Begin to draw your attention to your own body. Slowly begin to notice the place where your body makes contact with the floor, with the chair. And breathe. Notice especially the little places where you can feel the transition in that contact, the very edges of the place on your back that's touching the chair. See if, in your mind's eye, you can trace that very edge. See if you can begin to notice the very small details in sensation that tell you this part is touching, that is not. And breathe.

And now I'd like to draw your attention to your own hands. I'd like you to start to notice the temperature of your hands. Maybe you can notice that some places on your hands are a little warmer than other places. See if you can notice the little details of sensation of those transitions from places that are a little warmer to places that are a little cooler on the skin of your own hands. And breathe.

See if you can notice the sensation of your blood pulsing in your hands. Notice just where in your hands you can feel that. Now I'd like you to take just a couple of nice slow breaths where you notice the details of the inflow and outflow of your own breath. Let your lungs fill completely and empty completely.

Now I'd like you to imagine that in front of you there is a file cabinet. Now imagine that you open the drawer and reach in and withdraw a picture—a picture of you during that sweet moment. Let yourself draw that picture up from the file cabinet and feel it in your hands. Let yourself look into that face of yours in that picture and let yourself notice the details surrounding you. Notice the look on your face. And now I want you to imagine as if your awareness were some sort of liquid that could be poured into that you in that picture. So imagine that now you are beginning to pour into the skin of that you in that picture at that very moment. See if you can let yourself emerge in that place at that particular moment. You can imagine opening your eyes in that place and kind of let yourself see what you see there. Let yourself notice the sensations that you feel on your own skin in that place. If you're imagining yourself outdoors, perhaps you feel a slight breeze. If you're with someone in that picture, you might feel the warmth of his skin against you, the scent of her hair. Let it be as if you could just breathe that moment in, as if each breath just filled you with the sweetness of that. Let it be as if every cell in your body can feel what it is to be in that place.

Just take a moment to luxuriate in that presence. And now I'm going to ask you to gently, gently let your eyes open. Let yourself settle into that moment of sweetness. Allow the moment to keep pouring over you like water from a jar.

When you're ready, I want you to gently, gently begin to write down what you're experiencing, what you're seeing as you let yourself fill up with this moment of sweetness. Hear, feel, and see that sweet moment. Stay with it. Keep writing. Keep going until your hand cramps or you feel like you've run out of things to write.

Now I'm going to ask you to stop writing, but see if you can just let that sweetness continue to pour from you. I want you to notice if you felt any urgency while writing to explain yourself, any push, any effort. I'll ask you to gently notice that and let go of that effort. Now keep writing below. Just let it come from you. Just let it flow.

Once again, gently, gently let yourself go still. Put down your pen or pencil. Keep feeling that moment of sweetness. Now I'm going to ask you to gently close your eyes for just a moment. Stay with your sweet moment. Just let yourself see it. And let yourself be poured into that moment until you can feel it in your very skin and your breath. And then, when you're ready, just gently, gently open your eyes. I want you to go gently as if you were walking through a forest. If you walk very quietly, you might see things that you would miss if you hurried. And when you're ready, let your attention come back to the room.

◀

Accepting the Fact That Thoughts Are Just Thoughts

You've covered a lot of ground. Of the six facets of psychological flexibility, we've now introduced you to three. What's up next is the idea that you can learn to hold the stories that make up your experience of the world lightly, that you don't necessarily need to believe everything you think. In ACT, we call this *defusion*, and it is the subject of our next chapter.

AA and the Gift of Acceptance

Acceptance is a huge part of AA. One of the most frequently quoted stories from the AA Big Book is from the chapter entitled "Acceptance Was the Answer":

> And acceptance is the answer to *all* my problems today. When I am disturbed, it is because I find some person, place, thing, or situation—some fact of my life—unacceptable to me, and I can find no serenity until I accept that person, place, thing, or situation as being exactly the way it is supposed to be at this moment. Nothing, absolutely nothing, happens in God's world by mistake. Until I could accept my alcoholism, I could not stay sober; unless I accept life completely on life's terms, I cannot be happy. I need to concentrate not so much on what needs to be changed in the world as on what needs to be changed in me and in my attitudes. (AA 417)

You may find yourself sitting in an AA meeting and hearing the short version: "And acceptance is the answer to *all* my problems today" or an even shorter version, where the member simply says "page 417." If you hear "page 417," that means that acceptance might be a good direction to look in your life. This line has been repeated for generations in AA. In fact, you might hear a real old-timer at AA say, "Page 449" and then pass with no further comment. If you do, they are still reading out of an older edition of the book where the same line occurred on page 449. This story has stayed relevant and meaningful for many, many alcoholics.

And in AA, just as in ACT, acceptance does not mean liking, agreeing, wanting, or cosigning in any fashion. Acceptance does not mean sit like a lump and do nothing. If you think that, listen to the AA sayings like "God provides the vegetables, but you have to do your own cooking." Why do they say that? They say it because AA is an *into-action* program. They are affirming a faith that what is needed for the creation of a life worth living is available to us and that steadfast nonacceptance blocks access. Notice that page 417 is not saying that all fault lies with the one it refers to. What it is saying quite directly is that "I need to concentrate not so much on what needs to be changed in the world as on what needs to be changed in me and in my attitudes." This is not the same as saying all is fine with the world. It is rather a prescription for focusing attention.

The flip side of acceptance is often resentment. Resentment is one of the long-smoldering versions of nonacceptance. As the old AA saying goes: "Resentment is like taking poison and waiting for the other guy to die." Sometimes we nurse resentments for years, decades even. Sometimes the resented person does not even know about it, but we do and suffer the cost. The AA Big Book has some very remarkable things to say about resentment. "Resentment is the 'number one' offender. It destroys more alcoholics than anything else" (AA, 64). It goes on to say, in the fourth-step inventory of resentments, that "this world and its people were often quite wrong. To conclude that others were wrong was as far as most of us got. The usual outcome was that people continued to wrong us and we stayed sore.... We began to see that the world and its people really dominated us. In that state, the wrong-doing of others, fancied or real, had the power to actually kill" (AA, 66). Many people spend years grinding over and over the wrongs committed against them. We often feel compelled to justify our resentment. If we can get anyone to listen, we try to enlist them to join us in the resentment. Look closely at your own resentments and see if it is not so. See if it is not the case that, even in the midst of a well-enjoyed rage over a resented wrong, the "victory" is short lived. It is also worth noting that all that effort spent on whether the resentment is justified or not gains us little. They are suggesting in the above passage that resentments *fancied or real had the power to kill*. They may not literally kill, but they most definitely kill living. The Big Book suggests, among several other steps, that we view these wrongdoers as sick and suggests we offer them the same regard we would offer a sick person, even though we do not like their symptoms. This does not mean that we should stay in sick situations. Sometimes leaving is the healthiest thing to do. However, leaving in kindness does as much to take us from a sick environment as leaving in anger. You can choose to leave. You do not require anger and resentment to justify leaving.

The above also does not mean that you should suppress angry or resentful feelings. As we have said elsewhere in this book, suppression is a losing strategy. Keep working on your life, gently turn your attention to growth, and resentment will take care of itself. Those thoughts will come and go. However, if you nurse them, they are more likely to come and stay. Like birds, you cannot keep them from flying over your house, but you do not need to help them build a nest in the attic. In fact, resentment is only a prison to the extent that it organizes our life activities. Consider this fact. There is almost certainly a jail in your town. Does the jail have to disappear for you to be free? No, it does not. You are free when you are free to walk in and out of it. The key to being free of resentments is to stop actively nursing them and instead to adopt the posture taught in the 12 steps: "Love and tolerance of others is our code" (AA, 84). When we say love and tolerance here, we don't mean *feeling* love and tolerance. We expect feelings to come and go, like weather. But we can *act* in loving and tolerant ways even on the days when the feeling is far away. Don't fake it. Embody it. Embody love. Embody tolerance. As is the drumbeat of this whole book: practice, practice, practice.

The Serenity Prayer is heard at almost all 12-step meetings around the world and echoes the importance of acceptance in 12-step recovery: "God, Grant me the serenity to accept the things I cannot change, the courage to change the things I can, and the wisdom to know the difference."

When we are in the middle of a battle with the world, it can be very hard to distinguish between what we can and cannot change. A bit of stillness, a bit of perspective, and a bit of acceptance can make it easier to sort that out. The AA Big Book even suggests that alcohol itself is not a battle we want to fight. "And we have ceased fighting anything or anyone—even alcohol" (AA, 84) It is a paradox that even things we can change need to be accepted as they are *first*.

Just like with perspective taking, meetings are a great place to practice acceptance, practice love, practice tolerance. Meetings are also a great place to notice the harmful effects of nonacceptance. It is easy for nonacceptance to distract us from important life tasks. If you are trying to use AA as a source of support, try to let it be someone else's job to *straighten AA and its members out*. You will find plenty of flaws and flawed people in AA meetings. Don't let your objections to those people keep you away from the resources available there. In a certain way, you can think of AA meetings as a testing ground for living in the world. If everyone in the world has to think just the right things and say just the right things in order for you to live well—good luck with that. Use AA as a place to practice patience and tolerance for human frailty. If you do, you just might find that you are simultaneously learning to practice a bit of patience and tolerance for yourself.

5

HOLDING STORIES
LIGHTLY

Here's a concept for you:

    All of us are whole people and not life-support systems for a bunch of brains.

Brains are really marvelous instruments, but like a gifted child who has been praised too much, they get this obsession with being center stage. They don't know their own weaknesses, or perhaps know them too well, and they swell up in order to compensate, like giant puffer fishes.

You laugh! But just think for a minute about the kinds of thoughts that spill out of your brain at any given moment: *I'm a terrible person. I'm a much better person than him. If only I had gone to medical school, my life would be perfect. Why did I waste all those years in medical school, when I could have been a circus clown? Her sandwich is bigger than mine! Why does the sandwich guy hate me?!* It goes on and on and on.

Our brains are specifically designed to impose order on the world, arranging all of our thoughts and perceptions into more or less arbitrary categories and, when the information to connect the categories isn't already known, making up what's missing. The good news is that these big brains of ours put us absolutely and undeniably at the very top of the food chain. If you get eaten by a bear or a shark before you finish reading this, it will be because you were in the wrong place at the wrong time, not because the bear or the shark had anything on you in the way of cunning, adaptability, technology, or problem-solving skills. The bad news is that these big brains also incline us to suffer, to suffer over the fact that we suffer, and to suffer over our suffering at the fact that we suffer—not just any time, but often. Whew!

One of the more common general assumptions of psychology over the last sixty years or so is that irrational or distorted thinking is the cause of many bad feelings. This might be true. And it seems like a pretty good idea that, if your inaccurate thinking is a problem for you, the correct solution to the problem is to start thinking more accurately. The problem is, though, that the attempts to get people to control, change, suppress, or manage the contents of their thoughts have generally been unsuccessful (as we discussed at some length in the last chapter).

Getting into the business of managing your thoughts or feelings, including attempts to boost your self-esteem, in order to live most effectively is a little like managing clouds so you can live most effectively. As we mentioned in the discussion about self-esteem, there may be some level of cloud cover that's optimal for you: not too gray, not too much blazing sun.

Fortunately, there's an alternative strategy for dealing with unruly thoughts. Instead of trying to control and change the content of your thoughts, in this chapter you're going to learn how to hold very gently the stories about the world that your mind tells you—no matter what they are, no matter whether they are true. The more technical name we have for this aspect of psychological flexibility is defusion, which is a made-up word that refers to the way you can keep yourself from "fusing" with your thoughts much like your tongue would fuse to a frozen flagpole if you licked it on the coldest day in winter (we're just guessing about that last part—one of us lives in the South and the other in California.) If your thoughts are like clouds, defusion is something you can work on that will allow you to live your life in both heavy cloud cover and full sun.

(Note: since we think all of our thoughts are, to some degree, part of the ongoing conversation we have with ourselves to tell the stories of the world as we experience it, we're going to use the words "conversations," "stories," and "thoughts" more or less interchangeably.)

The Stories We Live By

Pretty much everyone on the planet has some kind of self-limiting conversation with him- or herself. Our goal in this work is not necessarily to make the conversations go away. We do not know how. Sometimes people spend a lot of time trying to decide if the stories contained in these conversations about ourselves are true or not. We are less interested in whether stories are true and more interested in whether they are helpful.

Take the stories that come to us from folklore. One of Aesop's fables tells the story of a man who was ill and dying. His sons began to fight and argue among themselves. The man asked for a bundle of sticks to be gathered. He had one son try to break the bundle of sticks. Try as he might, he could not. He then asked each son to take a single stick and to try to break it. They all did so easily. This story isn't true. It is a fable. But it's a very helpful story. The story tells us something about the value of unity. The story gives us advice. The advice is to hold less tightly to our differences, to turn our attention to what unites us, and to notice the strength in that act. The story of the boy who cried wolf for attention usefully reminds us to be thoughtful in crying out for help. The story of the ant and the grasshopper tells us to be frugal and hard-working, even when times are good and we're feeling flush. The importance of these stories lies not in whether an ant actually talked to a grasshopper about being hardworking (we're guessing not). Rather, it lies in the usefulness of the stories, the ways the stories help people move ahead in their lives.

And what about the kinds of stories you tell you about yourself? Are they true or not? Are you, in fact, a bad dad? Do you pull more than your share of the weight in the office? Are you actually the stupidest student in your classes?

From our perspective, the correct answer to any and all of these questions is "Who knows?" And an even more useful follow-up question would be "Who cares?" Unlike the categorically untrue fables we just mentioned, it's hard to imagine any useful ideas coming out of any of these maybe-true, self-limiting stories. Are you a bad dad? It probably depends on whom you ask. And regardless, "being a dad" is a verb. It describes action. Your action. In this very moment— and the next and the next—you get to do something that reframes the entire question. Are you the stupidest one in class? You know what? You just might be. Someone has to be the stupidest. But why did you enroll in classes to start with? To form opinions about your smartness or lack thereof, or to learn something? Do you speak up, participate, and reveal your stupidity of the moment? Or do you remain silent and allow yourself to stay that way indefinitely? The truth of the stories you tell yourself isn't really all that important. The issue is the extent to which you let those stories, true or false, get between you and a life well lived.

And what if your story is something like "I'll never be able to stay clean" or "I've been a drunk for twenty years, and I'm going to die a drunk." You see where we're going with this?

Wilson's Wager: Betting on You

The seventeenth-century French mathematician and philosopher Blaise Pascal had a wager about the existence of God. If God exists, he figured, you have a lot to gain by believing as much and living a pious and virtuous life—namely, you gain eternal life and a heavenly reward after you die. On the other hand, if God doesn't exist, you really don't lose all that much by believing anyway. On the other hand, if God does exist and you don't believe—well, let's just say there will be consequences. And if you don't believe and it turns out you were right, well, you get lucky: no eternity of torment for you. And there is the added wrinkle that you *have* to bet. In this wager, you can't abstain. You have to lay your money down on the table. If you put Pascal's wager on a chart , it looks something like this:

Pascal's Wager		
	God exists	**God does not exist**
You believe	Infinite gain (heaven)	Some moral benefits
You disbelieve	Infinite loss (Is that sulfur I smell?)	Some immoral consequences

Why are we talking about Pascal's wager? It seems that there's a kind of wager involved in how much belief we invest in our self-limiting stories.

If you have a story about yourself that may or may not be true—that you are the stupidest person in your classes, say—what are the consequences of assuming the story is true in the event that the story is or is not true? If you assume you're the stupidest person in your classes, you might sit in silence through discussions, you might not bother studying for exams, and you might not seek out extra help to learn the course material. Why bother? You're just plain stupid, and all your struggling and striving are just time and effort down the drain. You're going to fail anyway. And you do fail, even if it was possible that, with time and effort and help, you could have succeeded.

But what if you assume you're not stupid? Maybe you make appointments with your instructors for extra help. You might spend more time in the library or sitting in study groups with your classmates. You might speak up and participate more in discussion. And you know what? You just might fall flat on your face in the process and get ridiculed. Face it: calculus is hard, chemistry is hard, and there were a lot of battles in the Hundred Years' War. But you also might succeed, and there just has to be something of value to be found in that attempt.

So let's call this little problem Wilson's wager. It looks like this in a table:

Wilson's Wager

	Something extraordinary can happen	Something extraordinary cannot happen
You assume yes	Something extraordinary happens!	You struggle and strive to no end
You assume no	You waste your one and only life	Your life still stinks, but you get to be "right"

If you bet yes, you either win or you lose. If you bet no, you either lose or you lose. We bet yes, because no is always a losing bet. From where you are right now, the rest of your one and only life stretches out in front of you. No one knows how many days you have left. No one knows what might be possible for you to do in the time you have left. If you're reading this book, chances are that you've had problems with alcohol or drugs for some time. You might want to quit, or you might want to get your drinking or using under control. And for one reason or another, you haven't been able to do it. Can you? We don't know. You don't know. And each day for the rest of your life will give you only part of the answer.

If you've had serious problems with substance use, what price have you paid? Have you lost jobs, friends, partners, children? Have you hurt yourself or hurt others? Have you had moments when the best you could do was to lie very still in bed with the covers pulled over your head? If your life's a mess right now, you might not be able to imagine the extent of something extraordinary happening in your life. Your best-case scenario might involve staying alive until this time next year. Right now, what seems totally out of reach for you? A steady job, a home of your own, a loving family, a profession? It all seems so out there that you don't dare let yourself even dream and wonder about it.

And this is where Wilson's wager comes in. You can choose to assume that something extraordinary can happen in your life. You can do whatever it is that might make it more likely that this something could happen. Baby steps, we're talking here. Tomorrow, if you can't get out of bed, maybe you push your feet over the side and onto the floor. The day after that, maybe you can stand up. And when your time is up, the plain fact is that you might not make it. Like the prayer says: "Grant me the serenity to accept *the things I cannot change.*" Some forces are beyond your control, and you just might not overcome them. If you assume that something marvelous can happen—it might. And if it does, well, there is nothing more to speculate about here. If everything changes, you get a new set of problems and challenges to overcome. It is life, after all. But you'll be someplace you chose to go, and that freedom alone is enough to justify the effort.

Or you can bet against yourself and assume that nothing extraordinary can happen. If you do, and that chance really was there for you, you stand to lose *everything*—your one and only life and all the richness that could be a part of it. If you bet against yourself and, it turns out, you were right all along—well, you get the satisfaction of being right while your life crumbles around you.

The purpose of Wilson's wager is not to give you hope (and certainly not to give you false hope). The purpose is to give you the advantage of being a savvy gambler at the tables of life: your odds of winning are substantially higher if you play than they are if you sit out the game.

What would it look like if something extraordinary could happen in your life? Write it on a piece of paper and tuck it into the pages of this book or into your wallet. Whisper it to someone you love. It doesn't matter if it does happen. It matters only that you assume it might.

Sunsets and Math Problems?

Are you getting motion sickness from all the twists and turns in this chapter yet? Good. Linearity is overrated in our opinion. Holding on tightly to the story that things really do run from point A to point B in an orderly fashion is only a good way of convincing yourself that you understand something that's probably always just slipping out of your grasp. So, quick, look at the following expressions and do what comes naturally to you (no, this isn't a trick question—just humor us for a minute):

- 5 x 2

- 12/4

- $\sqrt{144}$

- (41 − 33) x (16 + 19)

Okay. Good. Don't think too much about it. Now, look at the following expression and do what comes naturally. Again, no tricks intended:

Okay, so what did you do in the first section? Chances are that you solved the first two arithmetic problems without effort. You maybe even knew off the top of your head that the square root of 144 is 12. Then, maybe, if you were getting sick of the whole thing, you saw the more-complicated fourth expression and you thought, to hell with this. You solved the problem of math problems by skipping them. Problem solved! Or you're a math prodigy, and you did it in your head. Or you got calculator or a pen and paper and you figured it out. One way or another, you dealt with each of the problems—because this is what you do when you're presented with a problem. You deal with it.

Now how about the picture of the sunset? What did you do with that? Did you solve it or figure it out? Nope. You looked at it. Granted, it was just a picture on a page or a screen, so you probably didn't stare at it for a long time in a state of amazement and wonder. But if you were standing on a Bahamian beach, with the trade winds blowing through your hair, staring into a sky that was on fire with scarlet and gold, you'd stop and appreciate it until the scene faded into night.

So, which are you? Are you a math problem or a sunset? That's right. We're not being funny. Are you—and everything about you—something that needs to be figured out? Solved? Do you even think of yourself this way? Have you ever had someone in your life that you just needed to figure out? Have you ever been someone else's problem to be solved? Whose problem to be solved have you been? Have you been a boss's problem to be solved? A teacher's problem? A spouse's problem?

Look, you're a born problem solver, whether you think of yourself that way or not. Look at what you did with those math problems. If you've been struggling with drinking or drug use for a long time, you've probably tried to solve that problem too, in a whole bunch of different ways. And how has that worked for you? You're reading this, so it's likely that it hasn't gone so well. You've tried hard, for a long time. And what would it mean if there was really no problem to be solved in the first place? What if you could just let the whole struggle go, just open your hands and let it drop to the ground? If you could do that, what might you be able to do with that energy you're not spending trying to "fix" something that was never really broken in the first place?

The Story of Me Being a Drain on the Universe

Here is a story about a "me" I thought I was and finding out, on my knees in a bathroom in Spokane, Washington, that there was a whole world that could not be seen from inside that story about "me."

Back in the winter of 1985, I was ever so slowly finding my way back into the middle of living. I had spent years living out on the very cusp of living and dying. Do you know that place? I was really just waiting to summon either the courage or the apathy to die by my own hand (but never quite finding them). Or, my more active strategy, secretly hoping that I would die by some bad turn of events—a beating, a shooting, a car accident—and living in a way that made those things very likely.

The first job I got when I got sober was working at a group home for folks with intellectual disabilities for four dollars an hour. The folks who lived there had to have profound disabilities and most had other factors that made them hard to place. Many had survived years in institutions, the enormous human warehouses our society built to house (or maybe store is a better word) people with these problems.

Just in case this starts sounding at all noble on my part, you should know that if someone had offered me a more prestigious and better-paying job, I would have taken it without hesitation. I did not give up wealth or recognition to take this job. No one was offering me a better job. No one. I was thirty years old and had never had stable employment in my life. I took the four-dollars-an-hour job because that was all I was qualified to do.

I worked mornings—early. I would go in and get the guys up and get them ready to go to the sheltered workshop. Because of the level of disability, occasionally the guys would soil themselves during the night, and then it was my job to help them clean up.

I remember with great clarity, early one morning, that dark-before-the-dawn winter of '85, being on my knees in that bathroom. All blue tile up the walls, hot water pouring down, and I remember the feel and the smell of that soapy, steamy air, and I am on my knees washing shit off of a guy's legs. And down there on my knees, it came to me, that if you could not wash the shit off your own legs, and someone would do that for you, that would be a good thing.

I spent many years dead certain that I was a drain on the universe. Getting near me would wear you out and cause you damage. The closer you got, the more damage you would take. Mostly people did not realize it until it was too late, but eventually they always did. That was the story I inhabited. I had evidence—a wake of broken relationships and personal failings trailed out behind me as far as the eye could see.

But there on my knees, in that steamy bathroom, I found myself useful. I had not known that I could be useful. And I cannot express how much it meant to me on that day, in that bathroom, on my knees, finding myself useful. And, now, remembering it all, my eyes fill with tears of gratitude. I have a special debt to intellectually disabled folks. Not an unwelcome debt, but one that I carry gladly. These folks with profound disabilities let me know that I could be useful. It was a gift of immeasurable magnitude delivered in the last place I would have expected to find it.

And now, more than twenty-five years down the road, I have received that gift a thousand times, all around the world. It has really been marvelous. Not painless, but marvelous and unexpected. I can't believe that I almost left before it happened. I am really glad that I stuck around. Really glad and grateful.

Here are a few things that occur to me, upon reflection: You might not be who you think you are. Right where you are is a great place to start. Let the world surprise you. Wonder what gifts might appear in the simplest acts and the humblest places. Never underestimate the power of a small act of kindness—offered or received. Take time to appreciate the richness of your own life, even (and maybe especially) in its tiniest forms.

Conversations That Are Prison Sentences

To recap—some conversations are prisons:

* Hold stories about yourself lightly.

* Let go of thinking about yourself and the others in your life as problems to be solved; learn to watch, wonder, and appreciate.

* Practice watching, wondering, and appreciating

And now, let's dig a little deeper into the kinds of conversations that you'll want to watch out for, the ones that are likely to cause you the greatest difficulty. People often get stuck inside certain kinds of conversations. We call these "prison conversations." We have prison conversations with one another all the time, and we have prison conversations with ourselves. Prison conversations have peculiar qualities that you can learn to watch out for. Just like actual prisons, you can get locked up in these conversations for years. In fact, life sentences are common. Any of these can be a sign of a prison conversation:

* It compares, evaluates, and judges (often dissimilar) things.

* It's complex, busy, and confused.

* It includes lots of "buts."

* It's adversarial and posturing, and it involves taking sides.

* It focuses strongly on the future or the past.

* It tries very hard to solve a problem (even if the problem itself is not clear.)

* It tries to explain the "why" of something rather than just describing it.

* It is very concerned with categories.

* You've heard it all before; it sounds very well-rehearsed.

Let's take a look at these in some closer detail.

Comparison and Evaluation: Prison conversations invariably compare things to one another, even when the things aren't very much alike. They make evaluations, and they judge things, saying this thing, person, situation, time, or place is better or worse than that other thing, person, situation, time, or place.

Complication, Busyness, and Confusion: Conversations can always be complicated, but you can count on prison conversations to be like virtual mazes for your mind to wander in, going every which way and doubling back over ground already covered. Be especially careful if you find yourself having internal conversations that include requirements that this or that problem needs to be solved before you can fully live your life:.

> *Why did this relationship not work out? Maybe I should have been more attentive. But then, it seemed like I was being attentive. And when I was particularly attentive, she seemed to get mad. But maybe it was the wrong kind of attentive. Maybe I was smothering her. I just never learned how to be with anyone. But how can I learn that if I can't keep a partner? Maybe she'll take me back and give me another chance. But even if she does, I don't know what to do differently. But if I don't try, it will never work. But I don't know what to do.*

So the conversation goes, on and on. Sound familiar?

Statements That Include Lots of "Buts": This is a very sneaky prison conversation, since it promises that if you just take the correct turn, you will find your way out. When you're having a conversation in your head, try to listen for the "buts." We generally think of this as a throwaway word, but it really means something. When it comes up, it's negating whatever came before it until whatever comes after it gets resolved. It's kind of like a verbal demand that something needs to go away in order for something else to happen:

> *If I don't quit drinking, I'll lose my job and my husband will take the kids, BUT I don't know if I can just stop.*

The thought *I don't know how to quit* has to go away before you can try to quit drinking. Your instinct here might be to try to argue away the right side of the sentence: *Of course I can. I just need to stop!* You can try to argue this way. Consider, though, whether the "but" here is actually something you need before you can proceed or if it's an excuse or a way of letting yourself off the hook for being unwilling to commit to quitting (more on commitment in chapter 7). It matters.

Fighting, Posturing, and Taking Sides: Prison conversations will often have an adversarial quality. You might find yourself waffling back and forth, blaming yourself and then blaming others for problems you've encountered.

Strong Future or Past Orientation: Prison conversations are usually littered with either warnings about the future or punishing statements about things that have happened in the past. Sometimes the warnings are only implicit. If you listen hard and ask the right sort of questions, you can hear the warning lurking behind what is said.

Just on the other side of "I can't look weak" is a warning about the future. Listen for words like "must," "should," "can't," and "have to," all of which point to the future. Listen and inquire for "have to's" and consequences.

Strong Problem-Solving Orientation: Like conversations with lots of "buts," the content of these conversations will present itself as a problem requiring resolution right now, before anything significant can move forward. You should be particularly suspicious of this when the "problem" being solved has been hanging around unsolved in your life for a very, very long time.

Strong Focus on What Something Means "about" You with Respect to Others: Prison conversations often focus on what something means about you in relationship to others in your life—or what others will think about you as a result of whatever you think are your problems. To check this, carefully listen to the stories you tell yourself: are you concerned with your problems themselves (*I drink so much in the evenings that I oversleep my alarm and wake up late for work*) or how others will judge you for those problems (*When I oversleep and drag into work late, everybody thinks I'm just some old drunk*)?

Explanation vs. Description: When you consider the circumstances of your life, do you think about them in concrete descriptions of events and experiences, or do you think about them in terms of explanations as to why these things occurred? For example, *I passed out drunk six nights out of the last seven* as opposed to *I got drunk because work was awful last week. I got drunk because I was fighting with my husband all week.*

Categories vs. Specifics: Overgeneralization, black-and-white thinking, and catastrophizing are all examples of categorical thinking. When you're caught in this kind of prison conversation, you might describe specifics, but you likely roll them up quickly into categories: never, always, hopeless, unbearable. Once you create these categories, they'll become "problems" you'll need to solve.

The Familiar (aka The Old and Stinky): Have you heard this all before? Have you been telling yourself or others this same story for a long, long time? Here's a little trick: try recalling how you sounded when you were telling one of your old stories to someone else or how an old, familiar thought struck you as it rolled around in your head. Did it come out fast? Are there certain "pet phrases" you use to describe something? Chances are that if you have been telling this story for a while, there is something in it that you're holding onto pretty hard.

These are not all the kinds of prison conversations, but they are very common ones. It takes quite a bit of practice to be able to catch yourself in the act, but if you can learn to do it, you'll save yourself a lot of grief over the course of a lifetime. Here's an exercise to help you practice.

◄ WHAT'S WRONG WITH ME?

First, take a moment and think about the thing you like least about yourself. Now, read the following statements—slowly, carefully, lingering over each. Read them aloud. See if you can notice some small (or maybe not small) seeds of some of your own prison conversations. As you speak each one, allow yourself to own it for a moment. Notice what shows up when you say it. What thoughts, memories, and bodily sensations come up? Notice how eager you are to move on to the next item or to skip this exercise altogether. Before you even begin, see if you don't have thoughts along the lines of *Not right now*, or *Sure, I get the point*, or *I don't get the point*. Notice if your mind is trying hard to get you to run the other way. Note that getting the point is not the point, though. Making contact, getting present, having the capacity to sit in hard places when sitting in hard places could make a difference—that's the point. So I invite you to do just that.

- I am selfish. I act like I care about a lot of things, but really I don't. *true*

- I am needy. A lot of people don't really see it, but I live and die on their criticism and praise. I will do just about anything to get people to like me. I can't believe some of the things I have done. *true*

- I'm not really very smart. People think I am pretty smart, but really, I work very, very hard and just barely keep up with everyone else. *false*

- I am secretly jealous of others. I get mad when good things happen for other people. I never say anything to them, but sometimes I say things behind their backs. *false*

- I just have to have the last word. It has cost me a lot over the years, but I just can't seem to keep my mouth shut. *true*

- I am lazy. Mostly people don't notice, but when they aren't looking, I get almost nothing done. I am a lump. *half true – leaning toward false*

- I am a coward, a doormat. I let people walk all over me. I get mad, but I never say a word. *false*

- I am unlovable. I have had relationships, but eventually people get to see the real me, and they leave. Sometimes I'm hopeful, but really, I know that it's just a matter of time. *false*

- Deep down, there's something missing from me. I've never been sure what. I look around and other people seem fine. But me? It's like there's a hole. *true*

- I'm fragile. *No*

- I'm bossy. *Sometimes*

- I'm ugly. *No*

- I'm boring. *No*

- I'm mean. *Sometimes — booze doesn't help —*

- I'm impatient. *Yes.*

What is it that's wrong with you? Pause and just spend a moment inside that question. What is wrong with you? Being weak means being shunned. Being stupid means being shunned. Being inadequate, boring, ugly, lazy, jealous, and so forth means…what? In the end, these all have implications for our current relationships, for the possibility of relationships, for the future of our relationships. And all we need to do is look at our past for that evidence.

If you are ready to run screaming from the room right now, welcome. We feel that way even writing this stuff. It rings our bells too! But hang in there with us. These seem so clearly to be problems in need of solving—what else could a person possibly do but problem solve? We think there is another way.

◀

◀ FINDING THE PRISON CONVERSATIONS IN YOUR OWN LIFE

Now that you've worked through our list above, here is a little worksheet you can use to make a list of the kinds of prison conversations you have in your own life. Take some time and think about each of the categories. Our bet is that, if you think carefully about each one, you'll figure out a way that it shows up in your life.

Prison Conversation Worksheet

Comparison and evaluation	How my drinking compares to others. My choices — to be an actress, dancer, rather than a mom.
Complication, busyness, and confusion	Spiraling thoughts — booze, marriage, finances, being able to save $
Statements that include lots of "buts"	How I've spent my trust. The decision to move to LA & study acting. (Rationalizing)
Fighting, posturing, and taking sides	The way Randi + Paul situation played out. Re-hashing / blaming.
Strong future or past orientation	Both. Mainly fixated on having money in life.
Strong problem-solving orientation	Marriage, friendships feel like probs to be solved.
Strong focus on what something means "about" you with respect to others	Fixate on why I drank — what led me to drink. vs. the amount.
Explanation vs. description	Both. Again, my general life choices. Feel I need to defend myself.
Categories vs. specifics	I tend to generalize.
The familiar (aka the old and stinky)	My upbringing. Parents with mental problems — continue the narrative. So I can't move on.

You might want to keep your list around someplace. If you find yourself struggling with a problem in the future, go over the list again to see if there might be some prison conversations in there that are tripping you up.

◄

Your Strongest, Most Imprisoning Stories about You

People carry stories about themselves. We're not really as interested in whether the stories are true or false as we are in how they work in your life.

Below are some possible stories. It's kind of like a chocolate sampler, except in this case, it's all right to nibble on one corner and, if it's not right for you, put it back in the box. Think about each of these imprisoning stories and whether they make an appearance in your life.

No one really understands me. All my life, no one quite got me. I always felt like I was on the outside looking in. *true*

No one really understands me, and when they begin to, they run. (This is sort of a variation on the above story.) No one really gets me. A few people have started to get close and when they get a peek at how I am, they run away. *false - the opposite.*

No matter how hard I try, things always go bad. I have had times when I was doing well, and I've fooled myself into thinking that things had changed, but in the end I always end up in the same familiar hole. *Attempting to break this pattern.*

Deep down there is something unlovable about me. I have really always known this, though at times I have been able to ignore it. The plain fact is that I am alone, and it makes perfect sense to me that I am that way and always will be. *false - I'll always have a partner. (but we're all ultimately alone in life)*

I am not very smart. I can't tell you how many rooms I have sat in where I was clueless, where I had no idea what was going on. I nod and smile, and later I study up. I spend my days sure that at any moment I will be found out. *false*

I am ugly/fat/disgusting. Who really could care about me? They see me coming a mile away. I am gross to look at, and because of that I never even get a chance. I don't get hired. I don't get invited. When they are choosing teams, I get picked last. *false. I have healthy self-esteem, if not pure vanity.*

I am mean. I don't know what is wrong with me. I usually don't even see it until it is too late. I say things to people that hurt them terribly. Sometimes I see myself doing it, but it is like I am watching a movie and there is nothing I can do to stop it. *Why?* I ask myself. *Why?*
I do in interpersonal relationships - husband, mom, in laws. I don't behave like this to friends, aquaintences.

I am bad.

I am not enough.

I am unlovable.

I am lazy. — *I am anemic which makes me appear lazy, especially in the past.*

I am petty.

I am weak.

I am uncaring.

I have a big mouth. *I can't keep a secret usually.*

I am a doormat.

✓ I am too anxious. *Very true.*

⌐ I am too depressed. *(sometimes) – however, more accurate is "I am anxious."*

I am defective.

I'm jealous.

✓ I'm stuck. *half—true – feels like it, but I'm slowly making progress.*

I am clueless.

It's too late for me.

I don't fit.

I am too much.

Add your own story that fits even better.

I have a lot going on. (Emotionally, mentally, spiritually, physically)

I'm always on-guard.

I present a facade – keep up appearances.

Image + being successful is important to (or at least to look that way). me.

◀ PRACTICE LETTING GO OF PRISON WORDS

We often live inside word prisons. Go back over the stories you chose and notice how easy it is to put in the words "impossible," "but," "always," "never," "must," "have to," "can't," "should," "shouldn't," "everyone," "no one," "right," "wrong," "fair," and "unfair."

On a piece of scratch paper, try rewriting a couple of the stories that speak to you using as many of these words as possible. Next, try rewriting them without using any of these words. You don't have to do it with all the stories, but try it with a few. Notice how hard it is to write these stories without these words. These words are the bars of the word prisons. They bar us from freedom to move in our lives.

Stories give us advice for living our lives. They tell us what we get to do and what we can never do. The "I have always been bad in relationships" story tells us to stay out of relationships, or it tells us to be super sensitive to anything that is going wrong or that might go wrong. The "I'm a coward" story tells us not to try new things. The "I'm stupid" story tells us to keep our mouths shut or perhaps to pretend to know everything.

◀

◀ OUR STRONGEST OLD STORIES AND THE INCLINED HEART

Take a look at each story that you feel attachment to, read it aloud slowly, and listen to the sound of your own voice as your read. Let yourself hear the sounds of the individual words. Let your eyes go closed and imagine what it would mean to you to let go of the story. By letting it go, we don't mean making it go away. We're not aware of any reliable way to make negative stories go away and stay away. Instead, practice inclining your heart toward the story, turning toward it in kindness. Let whatever needs to flow into and out from your inclined heart just happen. And breathe.

◀

Persistence

For the last decade, Kelly has been doing a little exercise at workshops he gives for psychologists who are learning ACT. He asks them a question about the thing that they like least about themselves—pretty much the same questions we just posed to you. He asks them to think of something that has been hanging around for a while, that has caused trouble at work, in relationships, in school, in their family, among friends, and anywhere else in their lives.

He has the attendees do a little meditation on that with their eyes closed for a moment, asking them to reflect on the places they see this thing cropping up in their lives. Next, he asks them how long that "problem" has been hanging around: One year? Five years? Ten years? Twenty years? Twenty-five years? The hand-raising follows a very predictable pattern: If you take the average age of people in the group, you'll get a smattering of hands up when the number of years takes them back to their teenage years. After that, more hands go up when the number of years is enough to get them back to their earliest school age. But mostly, all the hands will fly up when the number is just about the average age of people in the room. In other words, the things that we don't like about ourselves don't just show up one day later in life. They've been around forever.

After he gets the idea of how long these "problems" have been around for people, he hands out 3 x 5 cards and gets people to anonymously write down what these issues are.

What do they write? What does this room full of generally successful, educated people write about that "something" wrong with them that has been hanging around, most commonly, for as long as they can remember? Far and away the most common thing they write on those cards is some version of "I'm not enough." Sometimes it is "not good enough" or "inadequate" or "worthless." The rest are a smattering of "stupid," "boring," "phony," "incompetent," "bad," or "weak." He sometimes gets one in a crowd of seventy or a hundred who will say, "There's nothing wrong with me." Whatever it might mean to hold this perspective, it seems to be very rare.

Many, if not most, of these individuals will rarely if ever say anything to anybody about this story, about this deep and lingering personal sense of being flawed. If you asked how they are, they'd say they are fine without missing a beat. And if you look at them as a group, almost all of these workshop attendees—remember, these are all graduate-educated professionals—have and have had many of the things in life that their stories deny are possible: meaningful work, relationships, friends, and family.

Somehow though, logic does not carry the day. For Kelly, this raises one question: What if trying to make that story go away reduces your quality of life? In other words, what if battling with your own story leaves you less time, energy, and presence for the life you would like to have if only you were not flawed?

We think there is another way, and this is the way we're suggesting to you. You've spent a decent amount of time in this chapter figuring out what the stories are that define your life, where you try to solve problems that might not be problems at all, and how these stories might be keeping you imprisoned. What would it be like if you could just let go—if you could just step out of the fight? By letting go, we mean something more like letting go of investing in the story—investing your time, your thinking, your effort, your life. Like some crazy never-ending boxing match. What if the only solution is to step out of the ring?

Looking into an Empty Hole, Waiting for a Train to Arrive

This is a letter to a friend who was struggling with a terrible sense of emptiness. It was a theme that I myself knew very well, and I knew the struggle against it. It is my hope that this letter is helpful to you. What if the "empty hole" you find "inside" (and hate) is held in place by the struggle to not have an "empty hole inside?"

You did not cause the hole. Life just delivered it.

Or maybe you did
and if so, welcome, welcome from a fellow hole sculptor.

You are waiting for "feeling less empty" to arrive
you are wondering if "feeling less empty" will "ever" arrive
you are waiting for "wanting" to arrive
(wanting to go to yoga, wanting to meet a friend for coffee or a walk, wanting to travel)

you wonder if "wanting" will "ever" arrive
(other than wanting to want)
if that "different" "better" life will "ever" arrive
and, you are "thinking" that the best you can do is "fake it"
and wonder if you will "ever" be able to do "better" than that
...or if anything will "ever" change

"this does not bode well" you tell me

maybe you go and do things,
but still,
you wait,
you look inside for "wanting" and "feeling less empty" to arrive
but they are not there (inside)?

Only emptiness
and uncertainty on the "good" days,
and killing certitude on the "worst."

You are looking and looking inside for things that are not inside
(and never were, and never will be).
And are not outside
(and never were, and never will be).

It is like waiting to catch a train in the kitchen.
You look and look and look, but no train arrives.

In fact, you can't even see the tracks!
How will a train "ever" arrive if there are not even tracks?

But the "inside" you are looking "into" is not inside
inside you will find blood and bones and nerves…plumbing, beams, wiring.

What you are looking for is not inside
And it is not outside.

It is in the dance.
The dance between you and the world, the dance between you and living.

Let go of waiting for a day, an hour, a minute, this moment.
Let go of things like "other" "ever" "better" "different" for a day, an hour, a minute,
this moment.

Dance.

Dance and mean it.

Go to yoga, take a friend for a walk or for coffee, travel.

Be kind,
be gentle,
and allow wanting to arrive
in its own time.
and allow a sense of fullness to arrive
in its own time.

They will come to the party, but they never arrive first.

They come after the dancing is well-begun.

So dance, friend! Dance!

I need to work on this a bit more, but maybe it is done enough
for you,
for this day,
for this hour,
this minute,
this moment.

For now, much love, my friend, my friends
yes, you too
yes you

P.S. Your job is not to stop your attention from turning inside
(which is not inside anyway)
it is
to gently return your attention
to valued living
when it wanders "inside."

◂ EXERCISE: THE BOOK OF ALL THINGS

Pick a good big heavy book. Imagine your story is in this book. Imagine this is The Book of All Things. In this book is everything you have ever done. Every thought that you have ever thought. Every feeling you have ever had. Everything. Everything? Yes, that too. Everything. Spend the next hour doing whatever you need to do: brush your teeth, eat breakfast, comb your hair, but do not, under any circumstances, put the book down. Imagine holding it in your hands everywhere you went for a week, a month, a year, a lifetime. Imagine noticing how tightly you have held onto it. What would be hard to do? Also, you would need to keep people from noticing that you carried it. They might ask what is in it. They might ask to take a look. You would likely find a way to carry it that kept anyone from seeing it.

And, finally, imagine just setting it down. What might you do with those hands if they were not clutching that book? What might you see if you lifted your eyes from that story and looked out into your own life—into the possibilities that might be waiting there? What might you hear if you stopped repeating the words of that story over and over again? Might your life speak to you? If it could offer you some gentle guidance, where might it guide you? Adopt the inclined heart and sit with these questions. If you find your old pals worry and rumination showing up, imagine them as books and gently set them down—returning each time to your inclined heart.

◂

In Appreciation of Crashing, Bliss Following, Hero's Journeying, and Practice

Sometimes I have been asked about my experience with crashing. Because I have a history of the darkest depression, people ask me if depression ever visits anymore. It does not look like it looked in 1985. Then it was a really gory train wreck and would last for months and months and sometimes years.

Let me give you an example from about 1981. I was unemployed. I did not work much before my thirtieth birthday, and what I did do was mostly off the grid, so unemployment was my usual occupation. But this was a time when I actually had had a little job working at a community center. I liked that little job, though I drank at lunch, as was typical for me in those days.

Ronald Reagan got elected and the community center all but closed down with the immediate round of budget cuts. With the cuts, I was the first to go.

My baseline was dysfunctional in the extreme, but I had been doing well—for me. Anyhow, I got into this funk. My wife was working a couple of jobs to keep us afloat. Some days when I was home alone, I would literally crawl into the closet and sit at the back of it with the door closed.

I recall a day when my little brother came over. I was lying on the couch watching TV with a case of beer sitting beside the couch. He came in and sat down and said "What are you watching?" I had no idea. I hadn't bothered to figure out what was on—I was just lying there staring at whatever was on that channel. He asked, "Why are you watching this?" I shrugged. I asked Dave if he wanted a beer. He said "Sure" and I reached into the box by the couch and handed him one. He looked at me and said "This is warm!"—I shrugged. It just did not matter. Nothing mattered. Just lying there, smoking weed, drinking beer, counting the days, waiting for the end, but fearful it would just go on and on and on.

I have not been that funky in many years. I do still have times when I am down. Sometimes they stretch out a bit—maybe even weeks. But the funkiness is different—more permeable to things going on around me. I don't stop moving, and, even when I'm in a funk, there are times when I get engaged in things I care about and liven up. Richness can permeate—at least sometimes. The lows and stuck spots are somehow more flexible. There are some ups mixed in with the downs.

Before it was dead flat; life was a dull, draining monotone. There was no variation and nothing leaked in. The lows now are less sticky—everything that happens does not seem to get folded into the funk.

Why? Well, it all started the first day of June 1985. I said yes. I made a deal with the universe that whatever was on my plate on a given day, I would clean my plate and say thank you. So, if what was on my plate was depression? Okay. If it was fear? Okay. Or if it was doubt or guilt or anything else? I cleaned my plate.

Not entirely coincidentally, the last drink or drug I had (except medical) was the last day in May 1985. Drinking and getting high were my major strategies for saying "No" to what life put on my plate (definitely not my only strategies, but major strategies).

So the start was acceptance. And movement. I got up each day and to the best of my ability I did the next right thing. I went to work. I paid my bills. I paid my child support. I tried to do what a citizen would do—all new stuff for me.

Gradually my activity increased: first work, then school, work, more school, more school, more school, and life spread out before me. Engagement in life increased—broadened and deepened. I learned a little at a time to let go of what my head had to say to me about myself, my future, my possibilities, and the same for others.

Instead, I started using my values, not my thoughts, as a guide. In the Joseph Campbell series that I was watching, called *The Power of Myth*, Campbell was saying "follow your bliss." And he very clearly did not mean hedonism.

I spent a long, long time, and still do, inside questions generated by watching that show. What would it mean for me to follow my bliss? What would my life look like, over time, if I were to do that? What would I do in the next day, morning, or moment that would move me in that direction (even ever so slightly)? Will my next act move me in the direction of my values? Or away? If away, can I just let that go for another day?

Campbell also talked at length about the hero's journey. What might my own "hero's journey" look like? What if I let myself dare to have what Campbell called a "hero's journey?" (Even now, I shake a little with fear that it might sound pompous or presumptuous to call my own journey a hero's journey, or to even imagine one.)

Why has this changed over the years?

1. I have practiced coming back to this moment, right now. Heaven knows I have had a lot of opportunities to practice, having strayed from it so often (present moment).

2. I have practiced staying more open to what I feel and think (acceptance) without attachment (defusion).

3. I have practiced being in a continual process of authoring the direction my life is taking (values), and practiced letting go of rigid attachment to particular outcomes (defusion and acceptance).

4. I have practiced doing the next right thing (values and committed action).

5. I have practiced noticing (perspective taking) that this practice has opened up possibilities that I would never in a million years have been able to dream of prior to that choice on June the first 1985.

And I have failed—and I mean failed hard, hard, a lot, a lot, over the years, *and* I keep coming back to the practice. Sometimes sooner, sometimes later, but so far, I have come back one more time than I have gone away and this morning, this very morning, this very moment, I am declaring that practice to be enough...without justification, without consultation, without approval (including my own). I declare this practice to be enough. I expect my practice to change over time. How? Can't say. Will it change? I would bet on that. But for this day....I am declaring International Enough Day. Here and now is enough. This practice, cracked and a bit leaky, is enough.

I invite you all to imagine your own personal hero's journey. I invite you to leave the end of the journey open to possibility. I invite you to let the tiniest act—this day, this morning, this moment—be enough.

Finding Value in It All

On the trail of psychological flexibility, we've discussed:

- Learning to be still when it matters

- Learning to be flexible in your perceptions

- Learning to accept both the sweet and the sad

- Learning how to hold our thoughts lightly

Up to this point, we've talked vaguely about "richness" and a "life well-lived." In the next chapter, we'll take up more seriously the issue of choosing what it is that you want all of this striving and struggle to be about. We'll be discussing the idea of values.

AA and the Gift of Defusion

Although defusion, or holding stories lightly, is not discussed in particular in the AA literature, the sensibilities are common. The basic idea behind fusion is that we become trapped in and by our stories. When we look through the lens of our stories, it causes a lot of seeing and not seeing. Remember our prison words: always, never, impossible, everyone, no one. People often come into AA with a dead certainty about the past and the future. One of the things that happens in AA is that people get a chance to listen to many, many stories that sound impossible to resolve—stories of ruin and degradation, stories involving tremendous losses. We also find people who have inexplicably risen from the ashes of an impossible situation and found lives that are rich in meaning and purpose.

The fourth-step inventory is a good way to loosen your grip on stories. In the inventory, 12-step members take multiple different approaches to stories of resentment that have haunted them for years. The very process of changing your relationship with these old stories of right and wrong can have a dramatic effect on your ability to live in the presence of those stories. You do not have to determine if the stories are correct or incorrect, you do not have to agree with them or like them, you do not have to resolve them. In that fourth step, you learn to change your relationship to them. *In the end, you have your stories instead of your stories having you.*

Consider the following often-quoted passage from the AA Big Book, fondly referred to as "the promises." This segment follows discussion of the ninth step of AA, in which members are asked to set about a systematic course of mending situations in their lives in which they have broken with their own values and brought harm to others. Step nine is the amends step.

If we are painstaking about this phase of our development, we will be amazed before we are half way through. We are going to know a new freedom and a new happiness. We will not regret the past nor wish to shut the door on it. We will comprehend the word serenity and we will know peace. No matter how far down the scale we have gone, we will see how our experience can benefit others. That feeling of uselessness and self-pity will disappear. We will lose interest in selfish things and gain interest in our fellows. Self-seeking will slip away. Our whole attitude and outlook upon life will change. Fear of people and of economic insecurity will leave us. We will intuitively know how to handle situations that used to baffle us. We will suddenly realize that God is doing for us what we could not do for ourselves.

Are these extravagant promises? We think not. They are being fulfilled among us—sometimes quickly, sometimes slowly. They will always materialize if we work for them. (AA 84–85)

This passage often gives members pause. Stuck inside stories, these do seem like extravagant promises. But hearing these words sincerely spoken in meetings, hearing members who had indeed slipped far down the scale and have found themselves in the midst of rich and meaningful lives, opens the door to that possibility for the person listening closely to the passage. It creates just a bit of space between the listener and imprisoning stories. We invite our own readers to bring up the promises as a topic at meetings and to listen carefully for these stories. Allow yourself to become curious about the real possibility that you too might be telling just such a story of liberation, some years down the line.

Another aspect of defusion is the idea of not taking ourselves and our stories so damned seriously—holding the stories lightly. These sensibilities are often evident in the humor one finds around AA meetings. For example, a common AA saying is "If you want to give God a good laugh, tell him your plans." This may sound dismissive, but it can also be understood as pointing to the very human tendency to be completely certain about things that just turn out to be false. For example, most people in AA meetings were absolutely certain that they would never become alcoholics, are divorcees who were absolutely certain that they would never divorce, are parents who were certain they would not make their parents' mistakes, and so on.

Life contains a lot of surprises. This does not mean we shouldn't make plans, but it does mean we should hold the stories we create about our future lightly. Living one day at a time does not mean "don't plan." No great house was ever built without a plan. *One day at a time means that the plan needs to be lived one day at a time.* It means that we need to hold our plans lightly, since the world is a dynamic and changing place and if we are living well we are growing and changing. A plan held too tightly can begin with good intentions but end badly.

In about 1940, some members of AA were considering some rules for conduct for the AA members, and different groups around the country were adopting different rules. One member sent forward a list of sixty-one rules. Bill Wilson reportedly warned that attempts to impose even less grand sets of rules had failed again and again; however, as is the tradition of AA, the making of rules was not forbidden, since AA has no means to forbid anything. There was simply a warning. As it turned out, the member wrote back some time later saying that the advice had been right and that the sixty-one rules had been a disaster. The member also sent along a card labeled "Rule #62" that he had mailed to AA groups all over the country. It read simply, "Rule #62: Don't take yourself too damned seriously" (Kurtz 1991). Thus was born the AA saying "Don't take yourself too damned seriously." From an ACT perspective, this seems like good advice.

There are many other 12-step sayings you might hear in meetings that contain this admonishment to hold what we think lightly. "You have a thinking problem, not a drinking problem" points to a tendency to get caught in worry and rumination and to lose direct contact with your own life. It is, of course, really a warning against overthinking, not thinking per se. The problem of fusion is a problem of letting thinking about life substitute for life. In keeping with the oftentimes self-deprecating humor found around AA, a favorite saying is, "Don't go into your mind alone; it's not a safe neighborhood," and there's this version from Narcotics Anonymous: "An addict alone is in bad company." These sayings can be interpreted as negative self-statements, but if they are held lightly, and in kindness, what they point toward is the human tendency to become so engaged in analysis and speculation that we lose contact with the directly experienced world. When you hear a recovering alcoholic, sitting in a church basement at an AA meeting, say with a smile on his or her face, "My best thinking got me here," you are not looking at self-hatred, you are looking at someone who has learned through trial and error that sometimes their best thinking on a given day is a great source of amusement on another day. Sayings like "Don't intellectualize, utilize" are calls to action. Thinking about recovery is not the same as active recovery. AA is a program of action, not a program of thinking about action. Ponder, for example, the saying "The three most dangerous words for an alcoholic—'I've been thinking.'" As with the other 12-step sayings, even the saying ought to be held lightly. No one, and I mean no one, with an ounce of sense thinks that you should give up planning and thinking. But as the Serenity Prayer suggests, recognize the things you cannot change. And if you find yourself grinding through some thoughts over and over and over and over, and, yes, over—maybe, just maybe it is time to let go of thinking for a moment and choose some small act, or series of acts, that serves your values. As they say in AA, "Do the next right thing." This is not just AA folk wisdom; there is a substantial body of scientific evidence that shows that worry and rumination—a couple of very popular ways to get lost in thought—produce bad outcomes. And there is also a convincing body of evidence that suggests that moving your feet and actually doing things (sometimes called *behavioral activation* by psychologists) is very good medicine. In closing, on this little note, consider this AA adage: "In AA you live your way into a new way of thinking. You do not think your way into a new way of living."

6

BEING THE AUTHOR

Many people live their lives by circumstance rather than on purpose. They hope that things will go right and that things going right will lead to a rich and meaningful life. But what if the circumstances don't line up? At the risk of sounding gloomy and pessimistic, we've repeated this point again and again throughout the book: despite your best efforts, things might not turn out the way you hope. There is a lot in this world that is simply beyond your direct control. Sometimes life gives us a beating, and as we discussed in chapter 2, when that happens humans typically do some version of running, fighting, or hiding. Then they wait for things to get better. But waiting for things to be right often leads to long periods of disconnection and inactivity. Another thing that happens is that people have things in their lives that they really value, but they become distracted from these very important things. You can plan and strategize and take all the precautions in the world—you can even do everything right, whatever that means—and you still might not get the outcomes you're after.

If you live your life on purpose rather than by circumstance, though, you kind of need to set aside that circumstance-driven preoccupation with outcomes. You can choose the direction you want to head, intentionally and on purpose, and you can move yourself in that direction with moment-by-moment guidance. The world will do with you what it will, so it's never going to be clear whether you'll get to one place or the other, despite your intentions. But at each moment of your life, if you have your direction clearly in mind, you can do something that will move you toward it. This kind of purposeful life takes practice and lots of psychological flexibility. In this chapter, we'll outline the practice.

Another thing worth mentioning before we get going: From an ACT perspective, it's the values you choose and use to orient your life that justify and dignify the hard and difficult work you'll certainly encounter as you go along. This is true for all areas of experience, but it seems somehow more poignantly true in the area of substance abuse. If you're addicted to alcohol or drugs, and that addiction is robbing you of your life one day at a time, quitting is going to be hard, and moderating is going to be hard. More than hard: recovery is going to be painful. There will likely be times when you feel like giving up. In this way of working through these issues, the values you choose are those things to which you can hitch your star, as it were. When every part of you is screaming, *Why am I doing this to myself?!*, your values give you an answer: *Because something matters to me. I choose this life.*

Will You Let Traveling Be Enough?

I was asked by a good friend, "How long did it take you to get all this?"—meaning all this ACT and acceptance stuff. "How long before you started to live your life this way—consistently and serenely? Do you have a sense of how long it takes most people?"

I understand the concern, and ruminating on these questions is unanswerable, unhelpful, and assumes things about me, and others, that are simply not reflective of my experience.

Am I pretty good at this? Better some days, worse others. Better in some areas, worse in others. Generally better at it than I was twenty-five years ago? Sure.

I have never arrived anywhere, though.

Never.

So "How long?" is not an answerable question. Investing in the question "When will serenity arrive?" will produce little serenity.

Do you know what a new yoga practitioner does? Practice. Do you know what a yogi who has been at it for twenty-five years does? Practice. Do you know what a new meditator does? Practice. Do you know what a meditator who has been at it for twenty-five years does? Practice And musicians, and dancers, and athletes, and fathers, and brothers, and...

And do you know what a new ACT-interested person does? Practice. Do you know what an ACT-interested person who has been at it for twenty-five years does? Practice.

That's all I do. Practice.

Practice is like traveling. It doesn't have a destination. Think about yoga. Is there a single pose that does not have an extension, or another transition in or transition out of the pose? Or a pose that could not be put together with some other poses in a new way?

How long to arrive? Never. This is like asking how long it takes to get west. I am headed west. I am not headed to San Francisco. I am in the business of traveling, not of arriving. Destinations are illusion.

How long to "Get good at ACT"? Longer if you invest time and energy in wondering when you will "get good" or arrive.

In fact, about the time you think you have arrived, watch out! You are likely about to bump your head. They say "Pride goeth before a fall"—and they say it with good reason. This doesn't mean that you shouldn't appreciate the movement of your life in a direction you could love. It just means that you should stay humble and recognize that there will always be more traveling to do.

Why? If you are heading west and stop the car constantly to get a reading on how "close" you are, you will always be disappointed, because the distance west will always stretch out into infinity, no matter how far you travel. However far you have come will seem pitiful if you are comparing it to the infinite distance that stretches before you. And, those stops, if long enough and frequent enough, will end your travels.

Stops are not bad. In fact, good traveling involves pausing to reflect on the way taken and the way forward. But reflection is not the same as its life-sucking twin cousins worry and rumination.

Bottom line: Practice, and (my advice) declare practice to be enough. Travel, and declare traveling to be enough. I don't mean that you should cause yourself to "feel" that it is enough or cause yourself to "think" it is enough. "Enough" occurs in the very moment you choose to invest yourself in your practice rather than ruminating and worrying over your progress or whether you have your thoughts about progress all properly arranged.

Life isn't a destination. It's a journey. This isn't the least bit original, of course. It's the wisdom of the ages, and it seems to me a useful view.

Science and Values

We've tried throughout this book to talk directly to you about problems you might be facing in your life. We've tried very hard to leave technical-sounding stuff out of the discussion. In the area of valued living, though, it's worth mentioning that there is compelling evidence that living your life according to a plan of your choosing—that is, living a life that you personally value—is good for you. Active engagement with values is an important part of staying healthy.

For example, Cohen and colleagues in a 2006 study had students rank a set of values and write briefly about either a low-ranked value or a high-ranked value. The values were things like "being a good artist" or "relations with friends," for example. When Cohen and colleagues looked at African-American students who were performing moderately well and especially students who were at risk of academic problems, he found that they had a lessened experience of feeling racially stereotyped and that they achieved higher grades over the course of the study if they wrote a bit about a high-ranked value, but not if they wrote about a low ranked value.

In another study, done in 2005, Creswell had students rate valued outcomes and then give a five-minute speech about either their first- or fifth-ranked value. All of the students were then subjected to a stressful laboratory task. The experimenters measured response to the stress task in three ways: blood pressure, heart rate, and cortisol response. Cortisol is a hormone produced under stressful conditions. High cortisol responses are not harmful if they occur infrequently and for short periods. However, over the long term, these high cortisol responses make people less resilient and more prone to mental and physical illness. Although heart rate and blood pressure went up equally for people giving both types of speeches, the cortisol responses were different. Students who gave speeches about something they valued less had a larger cortisol response than the students who gave a speech about their highest value. So, even though the students who spoke about their top value became aroused during the stressor, the harmful cortisol response was far lower because they were engaged in something meaningful (Cresswell et al. 2005).

We could talk about many other studies showing medical, psychological, and behavioral benefits for values engagement, but the take-home is the same. Life is stressful. Recovery, in particular, can be a very stressful time. A newly recovering person may be making changes to many areas of living, and all of these changes heap more and more wood on the stress fire. The scientific evidence strongly suggests that active engagement with your values builds strength.

Think of values work as being like a good diet. If your diet is good, a lot of different illnesses may come and go. The healthier your diet, the less likely it is that, if you do get ill, you'll get as ill or stay ill for as long a time. Values work is like that. If you feed yourself on values, you will be stronger for whatever comes.

Values in Everyday Speech

Now, here's the part where we take a step back from the garden-variety use of the word "values." As we write this (in 2011), the use of the word "values" in American political discourse seems to have tapered off a little. For a while there, few politicians could open their mouths without making an overture to one kind of value or the other. And there are certainly lots of special-interest groups that have identified sets of values to which you might subscribe (or feel compelled to subscribe). Your community and family may more or less agree on a set of values it holds. "Values" means a lot of different things to different people at different times and in different contexts, and we have absolutely no issues with any of these meanings.

The thing is, *none* of them get at what we mean by values.

And sometimes people mean morals—a sense of right and wrong—when they talk about values. This is also fine, but again, it doesn't have anything at all with what we mean by values.

So, What Do We Mean by "Values"?

When we talk about values, we mean something very specific. It's not hard or complicated, but it is definitely a lot more strictly defined (and, maybe strangely, a lot more flexible) than most everyday meanings of the word. We'll give you a short definition, and then we'll walk through each of the parts of that definition:

Values are freely chosen ways you understand your place in the world; they are patterns of behavior that evolve over time based on your actions, and you feel satisfaction mainly by doing these actions for their own sake, not for any outside incentive or rewards.

Values Are Freely Chosen

This is probably the biggest way that our understanding of values differs from most of the common uses of the word. These are not anyone else's values. They are yours and yours alone. We won't tell you what to value, and we suggest you not let anyone else tell you either. You get to pick. While there are many preselected sets of values you might choose to subscribe to, for our purposes here you need to decide for yourself what they will be. If you adopt someone else's idea of what is valuable and it doesn't line up with what you really feel is important to you, you'll just find yourself struggling with another set of stories that don't work in your life.

Understand that the fact that you get to pick your values doesn't mean that you will always be a perfect example of them. If only. You may choose to value your relationship with your children very highly. Does this mean you'll always be the perfect parent? Not at all. Of course there will be times when you do things, even intentionally, that won't square up with your idea of what it means to be a good parent. Your basic choice to make this area of your life a priority is what constitutes your value (and we'll have more to say about pursuing your values in the next chapter on commitment).

Values Describe Your Understanding of Your Place in the World

This aspect of values might be a little harder to wrap your brain around. Think back to Viktor Frankl and his decision to remain behind to take care of his patients in the concentration camp. If you didn't know the details of his story—if you thought, for example, that he was just a guy in a terrible place who had a chance to escape and didn't take it—it would be hard to make sense out of his decision. Knowing how Frankl understood his place in the world—what it meant for him to be a doctor, a friend, and a fellow human being—explains and dignifies his choice. When we're talking about values, we're going to mean those ways in which you've decided to relate yourself to the role you will play in the world—as a member of a community or family, as a learner, as an artist, and so forth.

Values Are Patterns of Behavior

Values from this perspective are not individual acts. Buying your wife a bunch of flowers does not make you a good husband. A pattern of acts that show consideration, thoughtfulness, and kindness is more like what we mean by values. Giving a bunch of flowers on Mothers' Day or "just because" might be part of the pattern. It is the pattern that will cause, at the end of your days, someone to stand graveside and say, "he was a loving husband, and I will miss him so." In the sections ahead, we will ask you about the patterns you would like to grow as well as some particular acts.

Values Develop Over Time, Based on Your Actions

If you choose to value being a good husband, that value is unlikely to be static. Kelly, for example, has been with his wife for more than thirty-two years. Being a good husband at year one did not look exactly the same as being a good husband at year thirty-one. Being a good husband when he was diagnosed with cancer in 1998 was not the same pattern as it is today when he is yoga-strong. Being a good husband involved a different pattern still when cancer visited their house again, when his wife was diagnosed with cancer in 2007. Our most profoundly held values ask us to grow and change our patterns of living even though the central value remains constant.

This is another one of the ways in which our understanding of values differs from the everyday use of the word. Some understandings of the word might be written down into some kind of code. But our understanding of values evolves over time as the result of many, many actions you might take in the service of patterns of living you care about.

Another thing to keep in mind is that, in the sense we mean, you don't really "clarify" or "discover" what it is that you value. Rather, you construct it over time as you engage in a pattern of actions that, eventually, start to look like a value. There are certainly lots of snake-oil salesmen out there who have plans and systems in place to help you "clarify" your values. Take this kind of thing with a grain of salt. Once you decide what you want your life to be about, only your efforts over time can really work out for you what this actually means. And the meaning and pattern will grow and change over time.

Values Are Intrinsically Rewarding

Here's your lesson in behaviorism for the day:

There is a very basic idea in behavioral science that organisms (that is, people and animals) will work to pursue pleasure and to avoid pain. Pleasurable things are known as *reinforcers*; painful things are known as *punishers*. You get off the couch and go to the cookie jar, reach in, and pull out a snickerdoodle. Mmmm. Your behavior is reinforced. You walk to the stove, turn it on, and stick your hand in the fire. Ouch! You're punished for your behavior. From this point, you're more likely to go get a cookie and less likely to stick your hand in the fire.

For nonhumans, reinforcers all relate to pretty basic things like food, sex, shelter, and social contact. But because of our story-telling brains, humans can get reinforcement for all sorts of places. If you doubt this, try giving a chicken an "employee of the month" award or tell a horse that it's not going to get into heaven if it keeps wandering out of the paddock.

One of the basic qualities of a value in the sense we mean it is that it creates its own reinforcement. As we understand it, the act of being a good mom becomes its own reward, if that's something you value. Likewise, being environmentally responsible, being kind to animals, and learning to make beautiful music on the trombone can all be intrinsically rewarding, if they are things you value. If you only practice the trombone for hours each day because of the salary you get from the local symphony, yet otherwise detest the whole endeavor, you probably don't value trombone-playing all that highly.

You may find yourself in a place where nothing feels valuable. Please, please, please ease yourself into the stream of life. It is in that stream of activity, engaged in with awareness and flexibility, that you will find things to love. There are only so many things to love that you can find hiding under your bed. And moving around in the world can be hard, but we think, if you practice the things we describe in this book, you will be glad you came out and joined us in this varied and extraordinary world.

What Do You Want Your Life to Be About?

This may seem like a hard question or it may seem like an easy one. Either way, it is a question worth lingering over. Here is how we will do it. First, we'll do a little writing, and then we'll use that writing to do some wondering.

Keep something in mind as you go: It can be hard to make the choice to freely decide what matters to you. You might have had a lot of people telling you to straighten up and fly right for a long time. You also might have had quite a few dark nights to get to this place in your life. You might have a hard time imagining that you could really do anything in any of the areas you'll find on the lines below. Remember back to Wilson's wager. You might think that you are hopeless, but sometimes very unlikely things happen in this world. If you need more convincing, flip to the end of this chapter and read Kelly's personal story. Then let yourself wonder. If such an unlikely event occurred in your own life, what shape might it take?

◄ Sitting Inside Significant Questions

What follows is a longish meditation that you can do in a quiet place with just the book. Try to pick a time when you can devote half an hour or so of uninterrupted time to this practice. Or, if that's not going to work for you, you can pick up the thing one section at a time and mull it over. One way or another, you'll use your observations later to complete the Valued Living Questionnaire.

We'll ask you to consider different domains of your life, noticing the sad and the sweet, the struggle and the stillness. This will be, by far, the longest practice we've done so far. We encourage you to set aside at least thirty minutes of uninterrupted time. It may not take the whole time to complete, but having that protected time will ensure that you get the most out of it.

First, let your gaze soften and your eyes lower and see if you can just breathe in the experience of being here in this room right now. Sit up straight in your chair with your head balanced at the top of your spine, allowing your shoulders to drop and the muscles in your face to relax.

Take a moment and just let your attention come to rest right now on the gentle inflow and outflow of breath.

And if you find yourself thinking ahead to what we are doing, gently let go of that and notice again that in the midst of all that mental activity, your breath continues. No matter how busy you get, it is there, flowing like a river. It requires nothing of you.

Just let yourself linger for a moment inside that steady stream of inflow and outflow of breath. Each time you find yourself drifting away in thought, into the future or past, just let that steady inflow and outflow draw your attention gently back. Allow yourself to just notice all of the tiny sensations: in your lips, in your mouth, the gentle rise and fall of your own breath. Returning each time, you drift gently back to your own breath.

And if you find yourself irritated, wanting to move along, just notice that—that push—and imagine that you just gently release that and come back to this very next breath...and this breath.

Now you will ask yourself a series of questions about areas of life that some people value. Some of these areas may be very important to you. Others may not. It is not necessary that you value all areas. Just read or listen to the questions, repeat them to yourself, and allow yourself to sit for a moment with each question. Even if the area is not one that is important to you, just let yourself be curious about the question.

As you move through the questions, notice any thoughts, feelings, sensations, or memories that come up for you. Take a moment to breathe them in and out, then gently release them. These are important areas of living and we don't always pause and give ourselves time to appreciate them.

It's not important right now to answer these questions. Just imagine that asking yourself these questions was like dipping into a pool of water. Just let the questions soak in. And breathe.

If you find yourself drawing any conclusions, just gently let go of those conclusions and return your attention to the question.

As you notice your reactions, let go of the urge to understand them, judge them, grip onto them, or push them away. When you notice your reactions, just breathe that experience in, and on the next exhale, slowly set it aside and see what shows up next.

FAMILY

Let's start with the area of family generally—outside of marriage and parenting.

Read the following words slowly and let yourself settle into each of them, noticing whatever shows up:

- brother *alien, comrade in psychological family structure*
- sister *alien, passive agressive, guilt-trips*
- grandmother *old generation, stubborn, critical, aloof*
- grandfather *alcoholic, provider, enabling, head of family*
- granddaughter *spoiled, sweet, bratty, the result of families' decisions*
- grandson *heir of family name, legacy, pressure*
- cousin *different, foreign, rednecks, fat, uneducated, unhealthy*
- aunt *out to lunch, (no street smarts) wool over eyes, book smarts)*
- uncle *nothing good. glass half full, phony*
- niece *non-existant, pleasantries, fakery*
- nephew *same as above, child made by others' choices.*
- family *People pushed on you who you don't choose. Representative of "normalcy"*

Stress

Phony

Aliens:

Take a slow, deep breath and ask yourself, *If something were to happen in my life in the area of family, what would that mean to me? Are there people I would choose to reach out to? Is there a person in my family with whom I'd try to interact differently? What does it mean for me to be a son/daughter, a brother/sister? If I could be any kind of family member, what would I choose to be? What does family mean to me?* *Obligations, something to overcome.*

Linger inside of these questions, noticing any urges to rush through to the next section or to set this piece of the work down. And breathe.

And, gently, breathe…just settle and allow your attention to come gently to rest on your own breath before shifting to another part of your life.

INTIMATE RELATIONS/COUPLES/MARRIAGE

Read the following words slowly and let yourself settle into each of them, noticing whatever shows up:

- partner *business, challenges or is on the same page. bounce ideas, inspire, encourage*
- lover *nefarious, illicit, affairs, confidant,*
- couple *united front, twosome emotionally close happy, loving, togetherness.*

- boyfriend *young love, non-committal, wonderer*
- girlfriend *companion, arm candy, impulsive*
- husband *provider, stability, down to earth*
- wife *home maker, trophy wife, supportive*
- intimate *close physically, let guard down, share private info*
- close *lawyer – client relationship, transparency*
- marriage *work, struggle, ups + downs, institution, persistance, heart ache, deep bond*

government – romantic

Take a slow, deep breath and ask yourself, *If something were to happen in my life in the area of intimacy, what would that mean to me? Would I want to be with my partner in a new way? What does it mean for me to be a lover, a partner, a husband/wife? If I could choose any kind of partner to be, what would I choose?*

Linger inside of these questions, noticing any urges to rush through to the next section or to set this piece of the work down. And breathe.

And, gently, breathe…just settle and allow your attention to come gently to rest on your own breath before shifting to another part of your life.

PARENTING/SUPPORTING CHILDREN

Read the following words slowly and let yourself settle into each of them, noticing whatever shows up:

- child *beast, innocent, loud, too many bad choices involving children*
- father *distant, scrutanizing, self-serving*
- mother *mentally ill, bad word*
- mentor *necessary for growth, encouraging*
- teacher *passionate, helpful, inspiring, walking the path*
- son *dutiful, un-enviable, debutant, lost*
- daughter *rebellous, put upon, doting – (seen not heard)*
- student *everyone, of life, elective, encouraged in normal families, obey, by the book, rule follower, narrow minded – one purpose*

117

Not applicable

Take a slow, deep breath and ask yourself, *If something were to happen in my life in the area of supporting children or parenting, what would that mean to me? Would I give more time and attention to a child whose life I'm in? Would I change the way I am with that child? Would I stand by a parent who could use some support? What does it mean to me to be in a child's life? If I could choose to be or help to support any kind of parent or mentor, what would I choose?*

Linger inside of these questions, noticing any urges to rush through to the next section or to set this piece of the work down. And breathe.

And, gently, breathe…just settle and allow your attention to come gently to rest on your own breath before shifting to another part of your life.

Friendship/Social Relations

Read the following words slowly and let yourself settle into each of them, noticing whatever shows up:

Move towards friends who are in line w/ my values.

- friend listening ear, uncertain, wattling, enabling
- buddy dog, chummy, ~~take action~~, callous, travel partner
- companion dog, old folks playing games
- ally who you can count on, on my side
- supporter political campaign, money person
- helper needy mother, pressure on children, adult children
- pal helping hand- helpful stranger, distant friend pen-pal/on-line

Take a slow, deep breath and ask yourself, *If something were to happen in my life in the area of friendship, what would that mean to me? What does it mean for me to be a friend? To have friends? If my friendships grew and changed, what shape might they take? Would old friendships be renewed; would new friendships grow? If I could be any kind of friend, what would I choose?*

Linger inside of these questions, noticing any urges to rush through to the next section or to set this piece of the work down. And breathe.

And, gently, breathe…just settle and allow your attention to come gently to rest on your own breath before shifting to another part of your life.

Work/Vocation

Read the following words slowly and let yourself settle into each of them, noticing whatever shows up:

- work *monotonous, rat race, trapped,*
- job *conspiracy – taxes, lies, trade time for money*
- occupation *give your life to for money*
- trade *more freedom, creativity, autonomy blue collar*
- career *proud, lifetime achievement, prestige*
- vocation *where my attention goes, how I'm centered.*
- profession *more prestige, doctor, lawyer, white collar*
- employee *pee-on, dime a dozen, replaceable*
- worker *plebian, Charlie Chaplin, lemming, disrespected*
- employer *blow hard – power position, hold the cards*
- boss *slightly more impressive blow hard, creates environment, signs the checks*

Take a slow, deep breath and ask yourself, *If something were to happen in my life in the area of work, what would that mean to me? Would I find new life in the work I do? Would I stretch out into the work that I've wanted but kept myself from moving toward? If I could be any kind of worker, what kind would I be?*

Linger inside of these questions, noticing any urges to rush through to the next section or to set this piece of the work down. And breathe.

And, gently, breathe…just settle and allow your attention to come gently to rest on your own breath before shifting to another part of your life.

Education/Training

Read the following words slowly and let yourself settle into each of them, noticing whatever shows up:

- student *blank slate to be programmed*
- learning *something to do for pleasure, or jeopardy, acting – on-going, pleasurable, get more a method that makes –*

119

(Acting) — teacher helps them selves while helping others.

- school — *institution, prision for kids, brain-washing*
- class — *art/acting ✓ math/science - boring, mandatory*
- teacher — *under paid, over worked*
- growth — *always worth striving for*

Take a slow, deep breath and ask yourself, *If something were to happen in my life in the area of education, of learning something new or learning more in some area that I care about, what would that mean to me? Would I find meaning and new life in learning? Would I stretch out into the education or training that I've wanted but kept myself from moving toward? If I could be any kind of student, what kind would I be?* *Yoga retreats*

Linger inside of these questions, noticing any urges to rush through to the next section or to set this piece of the work down. And breathe.

And, gently, breathe…just settle and allow your attention to come gently to rest on your own breath before shifting to another part of your life.

RECREATION

Read the following words slowly and let yourself settle into each of them, noticing whatever shows up:

- fun *being at peace, oceanside, finding joy in being*
- relaxation *spa treatments, sleeping, meditation*
- play *theatre, acting class, board/card games*
- leisure *reading, parks, museums*
- enjoyment *being smart, contentment, taking pleasure, being right*
- hobby *writing — screenplays, short stories*
- rest *sleep, vacation, hot tubs, baths* *peace*
- sport *not applicable — for athletes*
- vacation *what I want my life to feel like*
- peace *an unattainable goal. spurts -*

place of non-judgemental

☆ ⅔ off the booze see-saw ☆ up + down periods throughout life.

Take a slow, deep breath and ask yourself, *If something were to happen in my life in the area of recreation, of giving myself relaxation or peace, what would that mean to me? Would I find new life in a hobby or sport? Would I return to an activity I've let go of that used to be meaningful to me? Would I stretch out into an activity that I've wanted to do but kept myself from doing?*

Linger inside of these questions, noticing any urges to rush through to the next section or to set this piece of the work down. And breathe.

Perhaps you can remember a time when you were very young and you played—really played without holding back, ran and jumped and chased and shouted. And maybe a day came when you stopped playing? Can you let yourself long for that play you once knew? Or, maybe, you were the kid who never got to play. Maybe you were the one who stood at the edge of the school yard and watched the other children play and wished that you could be like them. What would it mean to you now if you allowed yourself the gift of play? What smile might inhabit your face? What might play look like in your life right now if you gave yourself the gift of play?

And, gently, breathe…just settle and allow your attention to come gently to rest on your own breath before shifting to another part of your life.

SPIRITUALITY

Read the following words slowly and let yourself settle into each of them, noticing whatever shows up:

- spirituality *a goal to work towards, spirit guides, angels*
- sacred *bond btw. married people, vows, beliefs*
- religion *organized, rigid, valuable*
- faith *necessary for growth, guidance, forward momentum*
- holy *Catholicism – untouchable perfection*
- reverence *a feeling of awe + respect*
- ritual *a habit for the betterment of*
  ☆ reinforcing good values ☆ oneself

Take a slow, deep breath and ask yourself, *If something were to happen in my life in the area of spirituality, of building something sacred into my world, what would that mean to me? Would I return to a faith I've let go of that used to be meaningful to me? Would I reach out*

121

for the spiritual practice that I've wanted but kept myself from moving toward? If I could be any kind of spiritual person, what kind of person would I choose to be?

Linger inside of these questions, noticing any urges to rush through to the next section or to set this piece of the work down. And breathe.

And, gently, breathe…just settle and allow your attention to come gently to rest on your own breath before shifting to another part of your life.

COMMUNITY LIFE

Read the following words slowly and let yourself settle into each of them, noticing whatever shows up:

[handwritten left margin: part of the world helpful to others]

- community *[handwritten: support system, like-minded, empathizing, group-think,]*
- group — *[handwritten: lacking individuality or smaller aspect of community disagreement]*
- club – *[handwritten: exclusive, secretive, old money]*
- member — *[handwritten: key holder, special, important, self-important]*
- *[handwritten left margin: proud responsible]* citizen – *[handwritten: belonging to a country, area of]*
- *[handwritten left margin: (friendly)]* neighbor – *[handwritten: aquataince, pleasant, geography]*
- helper – *[handwritten: immediate generally good natured (real) cringe to the word "help" secretive, fake]*
- *[handwritten left margin: necessary for growth, change, healing]* volunteer – *[handwritten: self-less, best of humanity, do-gooders]*
- representative – *[handwritten: sending the best, physical embodiment of the]*
- resident – *[handwritten: similar to citizen, belonging to a smaller community cause]*

Take a slow, deep breath and ask yourself, *If something were to happen in my life in the area of my community, what would that mean to me? Would I find a new group of people that represent the things I do or believe? Would I turn back to a group I was active with in the past? If I could choose to be any kind of community member, what kind would I be?*

Linger inside of these questions, noticing any urges to rush through to the next section or to set this piece of the work down. And breathe

And, gently, breathe…just settle and allow your attention to come gently to rest on your own breath before shifting to another part of your life.

HEALTH AND SELF-CARE

Read the following words slowly and let yourself settle into each of them, noticing whatever shows up:

- healthy *extremely important, mind, body, spirit good nutrition, vibrant physically*
- fit — *self-care, capable, self-esteem*
- strong *resilient, mind over matter confident*
- well *mentally well, solid, doesn't over think*
- alive *vigourous, purposeful, intentional, magnetic — Tony Robbins*
- energetic — *enviable, stamina, boundless,*
- vigorous *too much, reel back a little over my level of comfortability*

sober important zest for life

Take a slow, deep breath and ask yourself, *If something were to happen in my life in the area of my health and self-care, what would that mean to me? Would I take care of myself in a way I never have before? Would I set down something I do that hurts me? If I were to treat my own body with love and kindness, what might that look like? If I could choose to be a caretaker of my body, what kind would I be?*

Linger inside of these questions, noticing any urges to rush through to the next section or to set this piece of the work down. And breathe. And, gently, breathe...just settle and allow your attention to come gently to rest on your own breath before shifting to another part of your life.

THE ENVIRONMENT *caretaker of abandoned/neglected animals, esp. dogs.*

Read the following words slowly and let yourself settle into each of them, noticing whatever shows up:

- nature *peace, beauty, centeredness. re-set. Adam & Eve*
- Earth *grounded, all encompassing, mysterious*
- the environment *shapes you, outside reflect inside, can trigger or support*
- ecosystems *naturally occuring phenomena happening all around us*
- life - *spirituality, discovery, life beyond humanity growth, precious, sacred*
- sustainability *government, interference, differing opinions, fragile, on unsteady ground.*

123

Take a slow, deep breath and ask yourself, *If something were to happen in my life in the area of my relationship with the environment, what would that mean to me? Would I care for the Earth in a way I never have before? Would I let go of things that I do that damage the environment? If I could choose to be a caretaker of the world around me, what kind would I choose to be?*

Linger inside of these questions, noticing any urges to rush through to the next section or to set this piece of the work down. And breathe.

And, gently, breathe…just settle and allow your attention to come gently to rest on your own breath before shifting to another part of your life.

BEAUTY/THE ARTS

Read the following words slowly and let yourself settle into each of them, noticing whatever shows up:

- beauty *of utmost importance, maintenance, fleeting, in the eye of the beholder.*
- art *breath, expression, awe-inspiring, glimpse at history*
- theatre *joy, my calling, exploration, expression, both getting out of my self/self-discovery.*
- music *classical, memories, repetition, tone, setting*
- literature *revered, great minds, writers, mental illness, alcoholism, opinions,*
- creativity *child-like, second nature, slant, smothered out of you, demonized, imagination,*
- appreciation *sincerity, by society, human. generosity, better people than me, condition*
- expression *confidence, self-less sure in oneself, taking a stance, unconcerned w/*

angelic

demonic

screwed up !!

consequences,

Take a slow, deep breath and ask yourself, *If something were to happen in my life in the area of my relationship with beauty and the arts, what would that mean to me? Would I look at the world a little differently than I have been? Would I take more time for creative expression? If I could choose to see, appreciate, and express the beauty of the world around me, how would I choose to do that?*

Linger inside of these questions, noticing any urges to rush through to the next section or to set this piece of the work down. And breathe.

And, gently, breathe…just settle and allow your attention to come gently to rest on your own breath.

Where I come alive the most — this section. I have the most to say, & feel. I have the most positive emotions & wounds around these words.

CONCLUSION

Let your awareness touch once more on each of these areas: intimate relations, parenting, family, friendship, work, education, recreation, spirituality, community, self-care, the environment, and the arts.

Notice any urges to skip certain areas of life or to rush through the end of this practice. See if you can't breathe that urge in and out. Without opening your eyes, call your attention gently back to your own body here in this room right now.

Take just a few minutes to write about what shows up for you as the most important thing or things in your life and why this is important and meaningful to you. Write your deepest thoughts and feelings about this area of living. What you write does not have to be grammatically correct. Don't worry about spelling or even necessarily writing in complete sentences.

Now set your timer for ten minutes. Please write for the entire ten minutes. If you cannot think of what else you might say, just rewrite the last thing you wrote over and over until something new comes up. If you run out of room in this book, continue on a separate sheet of paper.

Family was mostly negative. Doing that work kept me from visiting this Xmas. Friendships feel dis-genuine & unsteady or distrustworthy. Looking forward to growing my sober network. Work/Education also feels like a sham & the result of a government designed to control & produce. Recreation feels under-developed - it's a chore to be "at rest." I lean towards craving spirituality & community, contentment & want those areas to expand. Self-care is #1 & I strive for that most. It is the foundation for everything else. Environment feels ethereal & out of reach. The arts is where my heart & soul live and thrive. I feel most drawn to the

Not that you've spent some time wondering about these areas of your life, we're going to ask you to fill out the questionnaire below. Take time filling it out, but don't get stuck. If you come to parts where you feel stuck, move on and come back to them. And don't worry about giving the "wrong" answer. This is about your life. You will not turn this in and have someone correct it. You will, in all likelihood, come back and change things as you practice. Remember, this is about cultivating patterns that grow and develop over time. Just make a start, however small, and offer yourself the kindness of letting that be enough for today. The questionnaire is the beginning of a conversation with life, not the end.

◄ The Valued Living Questionnaire (VLQ-2)

Below are twelve areas of life that are valued by some people. We are concerned with your quality of life in each of these areas. You'll rate several aspects in regard to each area. Ask yourself the following questions when you make ratings in each area. Not everyone will value all of these areas, or value all areas the same. Rate each area according to your own personal view of it.

Possibility: How possible is it that something very meaningful could happen in this area of your life? Rate how possible you think it is on a scale of 1 to 10; 1 means that it isn't at all possible and 10 means that it is very possible.

Current importance: How important is this area at this time in your life? Rate the importance on a scale of 1 to 10; 1 means the area isn't at all important and 10 means that the area is very important.

Overall importance: How important is this area in your life as a whole? Rate the importance on a scale of 1 to 10; 1 means that the area isn't at all important and 10 means that the area is very important.

Action: How much have you acted in the service of this area during the past week? Rate your level of action on a scale of 1 to 10; 1 means you haven't been active at all with this value and 10 means you've been very active with this value.

Satisfied with level of action: How satisfied are you with your level of action in this area during the past week? Rate your satisfaction with your level of action on a scale of 1 to 10; 1 means you aren't at all satisfied and 10 means you're completely satisfied with your level of action in this area.

Concern: How concerned are you that this area won't progress as you want? Rate your level of concern on a scale of 1 to 10; 1 means that you aren't at all concerned and 10 means that you're very concerned.

Valued Living Questionnaire (VLQ-2)

	possibility	current importance	overall importance	action	satisfied with action	concern
family (other than marriage or parenting)	5	3	4	7	5	9
marriage, couples, or intimate relationships	10	10	10	8	5	10
parenting	?	1	1	0	n/a	4
friends and social life	10	10	9	9	8	5
work	8	8	8	1	5	10
education and training	5	2	5	0	n/a	2
recreation and fun	9	8	7	0	n/a	1
spirituality	9	8	10	8	7	2
community life (AA)	10	10	10	10	9	3
physical care	10	10	10	7	7	2
the environment	5	5	5	2	8	1
aesthetics, beauty, the arts	10	7	10	5	8	3

Now that your VLQ-2 is complete, let's use what you have on paper to do a little more pondering.

◄ WONDERING YOUR WAY THROUGH VALUES

Let your eyes go closed and picture yourself ten years in the future. Imagine that you have lived in ways that are very consistent with your values and that living has shaped your life. What are the most important values you have embodied in your life?

Try to think of at least one important value in each of these areas. What might each of these look like lived in your life? See if you can imagine snapshots of particular moments that exemplify the living of those values. The images can be quite simple.

Open your eyes and imagine that you could help your current self to live well. Invite stories into your mind that express what each value means to you. Work through each value and give a rating of both how important each value is to you and a rating as to how closely your activities map onto each values narrative.

As you do so, notice thoughts, emotions, memories, evaluations, and the ways these tug at you. Practice letting go of each as you bring your attention gently back to the value.

Making commitments is almost certain to call up a host of frightening thoughts, emotions, and memories. When these hard things come up, it will be hard for you to remain still. You're going to want to get busy and let your mind start chattering. If that happens, breathe. Use those moments as a chance to practice Six Breaths on Purpose. Use those moments to practice stillness. Don't try to push the hard stuff away. Just notice it. Watch it carefully. As you sit with it, it will start to pass.

If you are married, close your eyes for a few moments and recall the moments walking up to the altar. If you ever quit a job to take another job, close your eyes, let yourself get quiet and see if you can walk step by step through that process. What did you feel, think, imagine, and remember? Notice that some of your fears were "real" and some "not real." See if you can let go of the outcomes, and just notice the turmoil in those experiences. Events of this sort are instructive because they are clear examples of commitments. We ask you to recall them here in order to make contact with the storm of thought and emotion that often surrounds commitment.

Now, go back to those moments in imagination and see if you can notice your own thoughts in those moments *as thoughts*. Notice that in the light of knowing how that commitment played out, you have yet another layer of thoughts about those thoughts— that is, whether you were correct or not. See if you can simply notice those thoughts as thoughts too. Notice the emotions that were there, and the ones that you have now, and try simply welcoming them—old and new. And, finally, see if you can notice in their midst the you that was there then and is here now.

◄

In this last values exercises, we're going to try to get into something very hard: sorting out those values that are the most important to you. Be patient and kind with yourself. Before you begin, get ahold of a dozen 3 x 5 cards and a pen.

◄ A VALUES EXERCISE: 12, 6, 3, 2, 1

Bear in mind that this is an exercise. We'll be asking you to do something very hard in this exercise. We're going to ask you to imagine letting go of some valued domains of living. We're not asking you to actually give them up, simply to imagine it. Take a look at the valued living questionnaire and see if you can come up with a value that is important to you in each area. It could be one that is already a big part of your life or one that you do not have at all, but would like to in the future. Take a dozen 3 by 5 index cards and write on each card:

- One of the areas from the VLQ-2

- Some specific thing you can think of that you believe is in line with values in this area for you.

For example, you might choose the area of family. Write a few words about what this might mean to you: *I've always had a hard time connecting with my father. After my mother died, we seemed to find fewer occasions to speak to one another, and when we do, he criticizes me quite a lot for my drinking. I want to get closer to him and to make sure he understands how much I love him. This might mean that I'll ask him to go golfing with me a couple of times a month.*

If you cannot come up with a value within each of the twelve domains in the VLQ2, see if you can come up with more than one from a couple areas so that you end up with twelve total.

Now comes the hard part. Sometimes people experience losses in certain areas of their lives. Sometimes life calls us to choose to let go of things we value. For example, sometimes a friendship, marriage, or career is so destructive that we need to let it go. Sometimes this is true even when we still feel great love and attachment to the thing given up. For example, think back to the example we used earlier: throughout history during wars, there have been people who handed their children to someone on the back of a truck knowing that they might never see the child again, but also knowing that handing the child to a complete stranger gave the child their best chance to survive.

So, here's the hard part. Imagine that some circumstance arose in which you had to let go of half of the values you placed on the cards. Stack six in a pile that you hold onto, and put six into another pile that will get a sad, sweet goodbye from you. Take a moment with each, close your eyes, use your stillness muscle, let your eyes go closed, and let yourself see and feel what can be seen and felt as you gently release each one.

Mindfields: Your mind will likely get very busy creating justifications for why you release or keep each one. Or a huge "NO!" may show up. Your mind may also want to skip ahead and plan out all future choices. Your mind may berate you for choosing and not choosing certain values. Finally, your mind might tell you something about what you "should" and "shouldn't" choose and what others would think of those choices. This will be an opportunity to practice stillness and acceptance and holding stories lightly. Life is full of hard choices and this will be practice at choosing stillness in the midst of a mindfield. You do not have to chase these thoughts away. Simple notice them and acknowledge them—not their "truth," just their presence—and see if you can choose stillness and gently let go of each of those six values.

After you have done those six, repeat this process with three of the six that are left. Again, notice what shows up as you make your choices: comparison, evaluation, *no!* Gently come to stillness. Let yourself see and release each of the three values. Place these three in the pile of values you have already released. Take your time. Practice stillness and noticing.

Next, let go of one more from the three remaining values, repeating the same process.

Next, let one last value go, imagining you had to release all but one of the values. Especially, take your time with these last choices. Notice what your mind throws up in the midst of the exercise.

Starting 12 :	6 :	3 :	1 :	◀
Loyalty	Independence	Loyalty	Freedom	Creativity
Success	Support	Success	Creativity	
Freedom	Purpose	Honesty	Loyalty	
Creativity	Resilience	Stability		
Stability	Expression	Creativity		
Openness	Honesty	Freedom		

Long-Term Recovery from Addiction: A Story of Daughters and Redemption

Long-term recovery from addiction is a hard road. I have been in recovery from severe substance dependence for more than twenty-five years. My own recovery has involved a lot of three-steps-forward-and-two-back. For more than twenty of those years, I have had the privilege of working on the development of ACT.

I happened upon ACT (in a somewhat earlier form) in the late 1980s as an undergraduate. It came at just the right time. It is a marvelous thing when one's personal life and vocation can flow together so naturally. That is how it was with ACT and me. I was learning about acceptance in my own life. I was learning about opening myself up to pain in the service of what I loved. And, since entering graduate school in 1989, I have been privileged to translate that learning directly into the development of ACT.

Part of the tragedy of addiction is the costs to relationships. My own story is like that and I share it in hopes that my own story can help, in some small way, people who see no light and no possibility in their own lives.

Just so you know, right at this moment, I am sitting on my back porch, and I have my redemption mix playing, featuring Johnny Cash's cover of "Redemption Song" sung with Joe Strummer, just to set the mood. What follows is a redemption song.

I have two younger daughters who are a tremendous delight to me (Sarah, who is sixteen as I write this, and Emma, who's eighteen). They have never seen me with a cigarette hanging from my mouth. They have never seen me drunk or stoned. They have never had to hear that daddy would not be coming because he was in jail. They have never had to hear that daddy would not be coming because "we do not know where he is."

I have come home to these girls every night of their lives except when I've been on the road for work. When I say that I am going to be somewhere, or do something, they know that I will come through. Not perfect fathering. I am impatient, short-tempered, and prone to lecturing and pontificating, but on the whole, they have never had a reason to doubt that I love them, as Elizabeth Barrett Browning wrote, "to the level of everyday's / Most quiet need."

I have another daughter, Chelsea, who is older. She was born in 1975, during the height of my addiction. It is painful to even think about the risk I put her at when she was small and vulnerable and needed me most. In 1978, when she was this amazing, bright, tiny three-year old, her mother Elizabeth took her and left. I do not think she actually wanted to leave, but the plain fact was that to be near me was to be in danger. I was on a direct course for self-destruction and anyone nearby was bound to be injured in the process. Elizabeth did the right thing. She took Chelsea away and kept her safe. It was a difficult and courageous thing. I know that she neither needs nor likely wants my gratitude, but she has it nevertheless. She took care of our daughter at a time when I was incapable of caring for her myself. (I have had a lot of good fortune that way, but that is for another appreciation.)

I can still remember the day Elizabeth took Chelsea. We were standing in the dining room of our house in the north end of Seattle. There were rum bottles scattered around the house and people passed out here and there after a very long night of drinking and getting high. Elizabeth had a job and had to get up in the morning. She stood there in that room, with Chelsea standing beside her, and said something to me about change. I do not recall the words, but if memory serves, it was a last plea that I do something different. She had hung in there for five years and now it was not just her life in danger, it was Chelsea's also. I remember the sad little bewildered face Chelsea wore that morning.

Try as I might, I cannot for the life of me fathom how little effect it had on my behavior. Today, that face would stop me in my tracks. Today, the mere thought of it, the soft brown hair all around that small face, can bring me to tears. But that day, that day, it didn't change my course in the slightest.

I felt sad. I could see the tragedy unfolding. But it was like watching a play. You know that the next line, the next movement, will make the tragedy still worse. You know that the next act will make unredeemable something that has at least a tiny chance. You want to shout "No, no! Don't do it!" But the play continues. I watched myself light a joint. That was my response. This account may be wrong in detail—it has been more than thirty years—but it is entirely accurate in spirit. Elizabeth had to go. It was for the best. Lighting that joint was me signing away my last chance. And, in some bizarre twist of logic, I imagined that I was doing everyone a favor by forcing the choice.

Over the next seven years, I was jailed, in many car accidents, beaten in fights, homeless at times, sick, and sad. For my daughter Chelsea, I was absent. I took no responsibility for her care and support. I saw her sporadically. I think Elizabeth stopped telling her when I was coming because it was so questionable whether I would come or not. I expect she got tired of having to explain why daddy was not there.

It was very hard for me to be around children during those years. I could not watch them on television. I could not stand to be around other people with children. To see children, especially ones the age Chelsea was, put me right next to what a complete and utter failure I was as a father. I ran. I ran deeper into the dope. I ran deeper into the bottle. My consumption was crazy enough to frighten even hardcore addicts and alcoholics. I chased oblivion. I chased whatever moments of peace I could achieve. I did so without regard for the cost.

1985 was a big year for me. I have written about it in other notes. What happened that year is that I became so bone-weary from running that I could run no more. There was a time when there was respite in that last swallow at the bottom of a bottle. By 1985, there was no rest for me, only a bone-crushing certainty that the end could not possibly come soon enough.

Then, the strangest thing happened. That year, life got a very firm grip on my ears, and jerked my head out of my ass. And you know what? Once you get the feces wiped from your eyes, you can see a lot of things. The world is not all one brown mass. It has color and shape and movement. And, another thing I could see, a very hard thing to see, was that I had been willing to let a little girl go without a father in order to save myself from feeling bad.

I started getting back in touch that year. I started paying my small child support—every single month. I started doing what I said I was going to do. Still, I think Chelsea was probably scared of me. I was a big blank spot and her mother and stepfather Mark (another amazing blessing) were a solid and caring known.

I recall asking her to visit during those years, all the while knowing that I did not deserve it. I recall once when she was in Spokane visiting me, and knowing she so wanted to go home to her mother. And, I can recall thinking, *Who could blame her?* I did a faltering job for the next five years, trying at least to be sure that she knew that I thought of her and loved her.

Chelsea held me at arms' length a bit. I am sure it was incredibly awkward and uncertain for her. On my worst days, I knew I deserved only contempt. On my better days, I was less focused on myself and more on her. I think I knew how impossible it would be for her to even know who I was. I knew from Elizabeth that there had been times when she was very small when she blamed herself for my absence—how else could a child understand such a thing? I knew in my heart of hearts that she carried some of that forward into her view of herself in this world. How could it be otherwise? I did my best during those years to become someone who could be counted on, someone useful in this world.

In 1990, my wife Dianna and I were living in Reno, going to graduate school. I remember calling Chelsea on the phone and telling her, as I had many times, that I would love for her to visit. To my great surprise, she said "How about Thanksgiving?"

It was a stunning visit. I had been holding the door open for her for five years, but not really expecting her to ever fully walk through it. Not that she was ever unkind to me before that. She was always kind. In fact, I recall always being shocked that she was so nice to me, even when I relapsed into being out of contact. That fall of 1990 though, she came to Reno to see who her dad was—or perhaps who he had become.

That visit started a cascade of events. She wanted me to come to her high school graduation a couple years later—wanted *me* to be there. And I was there. I remember sitting in a funky little café in an old building in Olympia, Washington. I was telling her about what the building was like when I was a boy and it was Mottman's Department Store. She was smiling and laughing. And I was there. She wanted me to be at her college graduation. And I was there. And there was that delicious week we spent together not long after my grandson Fletcher was born. Usually when we get together, there is a bit of nervousness. I want to be someone she will like. She is nervous about the same thing. The result has often been that we get a little busy. But that week, because Fletcher was small and getting busy was not possible, we sat and talked. A lot. Sumptuous.

I have not been a great dad for her. Even now, her mom and her stepdad Mark provide incredible support and I am thousands of miles away. But still we have what we have—something that is of incalculable value to me. I think that she knows that in the clinches, she can count on me.

So let me finish this tale with an appreciation for my oldest daughter Chelsea. You see, she is the most amazing woman. And here is why. She has taught me about unconditional love. I do not deserve her love. My good friend Mick says, "If I ever get what I deserve, you do not want to be standing next to me." I know exactly what he means. I have not earned her love. And she loves me anyway. Back in 1990, she gave me another chance. Not because

I earned it, but because in her world, it was the right thing to do. She has persistently included me and forgiven me and taught me.

Although I am not a Christian, I have been persistently interested in a few Christian concepts. One is the concept of grace. Grace means unmerited favor. Sometimes this is interpreted as "You don't deserve this." As in, your deserving falls below the necessary level. There is another way to understand grace though—that is, grace is unrelated to deserving. It is not the sort of thing you can deserve or not deserve. This is what Chelsea has taught me about love. That it is simply not about deserving or not deserving. She has offered it freely and persistently and in the midst of that love, I have come to understand the meaning of grace. It is very good to know that, even though my head continues to say "earn it, earn it," my head is not in charge of my daughter's love.

Another concept that interests me is redemption. There was a time, years ago, that I was certain that there was no way back into life for me. There was such darkness everywhere I turned and I was just waiting for it to consume me. Since then, a lot of light has come into my life, but the light Chelsea shined may just have saved this soul. In this light, I have come to know redemption and to find my way to many other lights.

Chelsea, you just cannot know how much it means to me that you let me be your dad. Thank you.

If you are a person in recovery reading this, with a day or a decade: welcome, friend. I hope that you have found a bit of light in all this.

Turning from Values to Commitment

We're almost at the end. Having now gone through five of the six parts of our intial question, we thought we put it back here again. Read it now, and wonder a little whether it means something more to you than it did when you first read it:

In this very moment, will you accept the sad and the sweet, hold lightly stories about what is possible, and be the author of a life that has meaning and purpose for you, turning in kindness back to that life when you find yourself moving away from it?

We mentioned earlier in the chapter that just choosing a valued direction doesn't suggest that you will be a perfect example of that value all the time. We are pretty certain that you will fail spectacularly at living in a way that furthers any serious value you hold at least once and probably many, many times for as long as you hold that value. And you know, this is totally okay. The only people who do not fall down are people who do not get up.

The work we're talking about is this book is grounded in acceptance and commitment therapy. We already talked about the acceptance part. Now, let's get to the commitment bit. And, just as it was for values, we're going to talk about commitment in a way that, at first, might seem a little surprising.

AA AND THE GIFT OF VALUES

The 12 steps and ACT are similar in that they are really all about valued living. Both of these traditions are means to an end, and that end is a richer and more meaningful life. This is important to mention because in some other traditions this may not be so, and there is a danger that, even in 12-step and ACT, we might from time to time forget that it is so.

Sometimes, for example, you might hear someone talk about acceptance for its own sake, as if acceptance were intrinsically good. The same could be said about getting present, holding your stories lightly, and so forth. When these techniques are taken to be ends in themselves (rather than means to an end), therapy can easily take on the character of emotional wallowing.

That's not the intention in the ACT model, and it's not the AA model either. In ACT, we accept, get present, hold stories lightly, learn to take other perspectives and to notice the "I" that is not some tightly held story. All of these are done in the service of more effective living. And "more effective," as we see most clearly in this chapter, means effective in authoring a pattern of living that you could love.

In AA, the agenda is the same. Acceptance in AA is not for its own sake. Remember that "Grant me the courage to change the things I can" is also part of the Serenity Prayer. Even getting sober is not something you do for its own sake. It's not an end in itself. From *Living Sober:*

Simply trying to avoid the drink (or not think of one), all by itself, doesn't seem to be enough. The more we think about the drink we are trying to keep away from, the more it occupies our mind…Just *not drinking* is a negative and sterile thing. To *stay* stopped we found we need to put in place a positive program of action. We've found we had to learn to *live* sober" (AA World Services, Inc., 1998, 13, emphasis in original).

Notice how this AA text highlights the futility of avoidance and the virtues of actively authoring a pattern of living. That chapter goes on to talk about a variety of domains of living not unlike the domains discussed in this book.

How can you practice active authorship of valued living in the context of AA? Many of the AA steps can be hard to swallow. For example, an admission of powerlessness: who wants that? However, if you've struggled and struggled to manage your drug or alcohol use, only to fail repeatedly, perhaps you're one of those who need to "manage" drugs and alcohol by simply letting them go as part of your life. Think of all the effort you've put into controlling your use. If it had been fruitful in any lasting or satisfying sense, you wouldn't be reading this book. Now imagine that all the effort you poured into controlling use could be diverted into a value—one that you would want on your tombstone. "He was a devoted father," for example. How might that value thrive if all that effort you put into not drinking could be poured into fatherhood? How might you grow as a father if all the hours spent struggling, drinking, not drinking, worrying over doing and not doing it were instead spent on your kids? When you work the first step, consider asking yourself, honestly, do you really want your tombstone to be inscribed with "He struggled mightily with alcohol?" Or would you prefer it read:

- He was an inspired artist

- He was a great teacher

- He made a real difference in his community as an activist

- He was a wonderful parent, spouse, and neighbor

Could you let the first step symbolize a turning point in your life where you let go of that struggle with drugs or alcohol and put your hands firmly on your own life?

Consider the second and third steps and the idea of restoration to sanity and turning life direction over to a higher power. Some have said that the definition of insanity is doing the same thing over and over but expecting different results. What's the alternative? For some who are religiously inclined, or spiritual in a more general sense, God (as you understand God) can be your guide in this. There are no great religious or spiritual traditions that are not centrally concerned with what it means to live a virtuous life. Sometimes you have to sift through a lot of scary talk about hellfire and damnation to find it, but all of the great religions are fundamentally concerned with how we might live among our fellows.

But if you're spiritually uncertain, or even if you're an atheist, couldn't you add just one little "o" to the word God—making it "good" instead? After all, some say God is good. The third step might sound something like: "Made a decision to turn our will and our lives over to Good as we understood it." What might it look like if you were to practice the embodiment of living well, to the best of your ability on a given day? Could you allow good to organize your life? Could it be that allowing your own most deeply held values to direct your life might result in a life free of the insanity of repetitive, life draining patterns?

The fourth and fifth steps are most clearly about finding where we have gotten sidetracked from the things we care most deeply about. Taking inventory in the fourth step is a values exercise. It is largely a step about how fear, resentment, and avoidance have corrupted relationships—and, after all, most values are connected to relationships. "A business which takes no regular inventory usually goes broke...If the owner of the business is to be successful, he cannot fool himself about values. We did exactly the same thing with our lives" (AA, 64). Many components of the inventories we did in the early chapters of this book—practicing stillness in a storm, practicing perspective taking, practicing holding stories lightly—can all be allies in working the fourth and fifth steps with a kind but firm hand on the rudder and an eye toward the direction you are moving in your life. Let those skills carry you through these challenging, life-orienting steps.

Steps six and seven are about letting go of old, repetitive, unproductive patterns and allowing some force other than fear, avoidance, and self-defeating stories to organize your life. These steps can be a sort of reaffirmation of all that has been done in the first five steps. The first five steps are a process of becoming ready to let go of old patterns of being. The sixth step is an affirmation of that in light of all that has been seen in the preceding steps. The sixth step is an affirmation of the harm that has been caused and the path to better living. The seventh step in many ways echoes the second and third—freely choosing to have good or God, in whatever form that takes for you, orient you one day at a time. This is most certainly a values question: what will organize my life?

Steps eight and nine are also very much about growing in the direction of a valued pattern of living, but they are even more closely related to committed action, which is described in the next chapter, so I'll save discussion of those steps for later. Steps ten, eleven, and twelve are often thought of as maintenance steps. They encapsulate the processes described in the first nine steps. They are the "rinse and repeat" steps in AA. Again, I'll say a bit more about these in the next chapter on committed action, since these steps bear a very strong relationship to the meaning of committed action in the ACT model.

A final place to consider ACT values components in relation to 12-step participation is in the domain of community and social relations. Most who use AA as a place to practice their recovery become part of a community. It is worth spending a bit of time meditating on, and writing about, who you would like to be in that community. As in all ACT values work, hold your values-authorship lightly. Hold the story about who you want to be lightly. As you grow and change in that community, what is meant by "being a good member" will likely change. I encourage you to stretch a bit and move around in your role in that community. Spend a bit of time passing and not speaking, but listening with extra care. Spend some time speaking frequently. Take time to notice your place in that community. Do you walk up to a newcomer, shake her hand, and welcome her to the meeting? Do you serve coffee some days? Can people count on seeing you there—rain or shine? Are you someone who shares both their brightest and darkest days? Meetings are a good place to practice interpersonal values.

7

TURNING BACK,
IN KINDNESS

Here's the interesting thing about all these areas, these processes, that we've been talking about: stillness, perspective-taking, acceptance, the holding lightly of stories, and values. Like the facets of a jewel, all of them are reflected in each other. Take a look at any one of them closely, and you'll see the others. Maybe they won't appear exactly the same way, but they'll be there. None of them is more important than the other, but this work depends on all of them working together to foster psychological flexibility and, from that, the possibility of changing your life for the better. This weaving together and connectedness of the areas is the subject of our last discussion: commitment. You can think all you want about the stuff that comes earlier in this book, but all of it risks being for nothing unless you can get your feet to start moving.

Our purpose here is to talk about how you can take the ideas from the earlier chapters and, even in the smallest of ways, *do* something that will take you in a direction you want to go. Whatever you can think of, whatever you can manage, right now is the time to find even the tiniest way you can begin to take action. In ACT, we call this resolve to act *commitment*. The idea is that, from moment to moment, you commit to do things that take you in the direction of what it is that matters to you in your life. In other words, you commit to act in a way that is consistent with what you value. But, similar to values, the ACT take on commitment is a little different than the everyday use of the word.

Commitment in the Everyday Sense

When we use the word in our day-to-day conversations, we typically take commitment to mean "a promise we make to do something in the future." Whether you commit to doing something limited in scope, like showing up at a specific time to help a friend move, or you commit to something ongoing and indefinite, such as a marriage or the decision to become a parent, we understand commitment as a promise to behave some certain way at some point or points in the future. And we distinguish between keeping or honoring our commitments and breaking them. If you succeed in doing what you promised to do, hooray! If you fail, boo!

For our purposes, though, this understanding of commitment isn't as useful as we might hope. We'll get to what we do mean by commitment, but first, try this little exercise.

◄ CHECKING IN ON YOUR COMMITMENTS

Call to mind some little thing you could do. Look back at the values you wrote about in the last chapter and see if you can find a possible commitment there. You only need to think of one, but be specific. It'll probably come easily to you. If it takes a while, just breathe gently and wait for it to show up.

Once you've got your commitment pictured clearly in your mind, let yourself wonder about how it might play out in your life in a week, a month, a year, five years, if the events of your life go as you intend. What would it look like in ten years' time if you honored this commitment?

Now take a deep breath, hold it, and let it out. Start letting images gather in your mind of what your life would start to look like if you *didn't* honor your commitment. What would your life look like in a decade if you discovered that you weren't able to keep this commitment or if you just decided to walk away from it? Be careful. Your tendency will probably be to try to rescue or advise your future self. Don't do it. Just wonder about what breaking your commitment would be like; don't solve any problems you encounter or try to push anything away.

Now take one more deep breath and let it out. This time, consider your life as it is right now and where, to the best of your knowledge, you see it heading in the future. Let yourself wonder *whether* you'll keep your commitment. Don't try too hard to argue for one outcome or the other. Just wonder what might actually happen. Do you think you'll honor your commitment, or will you let it go? Pay very close attention to the sensations you feel in your body.

◄

Of the three little meditations, which seemed to cause the most noticeable changes in your body? Was it the third? If it was, there's a good reason, and it's called uncertainty. Will you honor your commitment? Unless you have a hotline to the future, your honest answer to this question is "I don't know." And the bad news is that, as long as you're still breathing, your answer will be either "I don't know" or "No. I failed." With open-ended commitments, ambiguity is a certainty, and you can only get relief from this ambiguity in failure.

Say you have an alcohol problem. After years of problem drinking, you finally decide to make a change. You go into rehab. You get the best education about alcoholism and its treatment. You assemble a team of doctors, therapists, good friends, loved ones, sponsors, and a meeting community to support you through recovery. And then you make a promise to yourself: I'm not going to take another drink.

Will you drink again? We don't know. And as long as you're still breathing, we'll never know. We might talk about the odds of relapse, based on the success rates of the treatments you receive. We might look at examples of commitments you've made in the past and make a guess about your commitment "credit score." But the only way to "answer" the question of whether you'll drink again is to watch each unfolding moment of your life—from now until you draw your last breath—to see whether you'll open another bottle or raise another glass to your lips. Depending on circumstances, you could be watching this process for a very long time. And all the while, you'll be swimming in—you guessed it—ambiguity. Many people in recovery struggle with this not-knowing, and there's more than a little reason to suppose that this struggle is behind many a relapse: In the moment you take that next drink, the ambiguity goes away. We get our answer: yes, you will drink again. And in that answer, even if it's devastating, even if it literally condemns you, you get a moment of peace, however short lived.

Commitment in ACT

We've devoted a whole chapter to commitment, and we've already told you that committed action is one of the fundamental processes that makes ACT work. But now we have all this business about ambiguity and the anxiety that comes with making promises about the future. So, what gives?

It turns out that there's more to commitment, from an ACT perspective, than just making promises about the future. While the everyday sense of the word is certainly a part of commitment in ACT, it doesn't tell the whole story. It is not even the most important part of the story. The most important part of the story about commitment is written in this very moment.

Looking to the Future, Acting in the Present

If it were common for us to always keep the promises we make to ourselves and others about our actions in the future, our commitments would be effectively synonymous with our values. There wouldn't really be a need for this chapter. You could just read the last chapter, spend some time deciding what you want your life to be about, and then you'd be in business.

But we all know this isn't the case. The narratives of our lives are made up of story after story of broken promises, of honest commitments made today that become the burdens and disappointments of tomorrow. Whether these setbacks are due to circumstances beyond our control, our own inability to live up to the expectations we set for ourselves, or because on that day we were unstill or prideful is beside the point. Whatever its cause, failure is a familiar friend to us all. And how do you feel when you fail? Free and easy and fresh as a daisy? No. You feel bad. It weighs on you. And so commitments—to the extent that they're promises we make to act a certain way in the future—may not lead us to greater psychological flexibility.

But what if we were less concerned with the outcome of these promises we make than about what we're going to do today? What if we understood commitment as something that we do in the present? Consider again what your experience with alcohol addiction might look like. You commit to stay sober. Will you drink again? As we said, we don't know. Only time will tell. We can't answer that question, but there are others we can answer: Are you drinking now? Right now? No. And what about now? Still no. Moment by moment, you can renew this commitment to not drink.

The understanding of commitment that interests us is committing to act in the present moment in ways that are directed by values. Sure, you can have values-directed goals along the way. We're less concerned, though, with whether you achieve those goals. It's great if you do, but it's not the whole story. This is because, sometimes (and maybe much of the time), we can't really imagine what's possible in our lives until it happens or is, at least, about to happen. Have you ever known someone who really turned his life around? Someone who went from rock bottom to a life that he was delighted with?

You can imagine such a situation even if you can't think of anyone off the top of your head. Again, imagine what could very well be your own drinking problem. If we took a look at your life, let's say, five years ago, you might be waking up on the floor most nights. You might be in and out of abusive relationships and unable to hold a job for very long. Maybe you wrap your car around a tree some rainy evening. At this point in your life, what do you suppose you might hope for? Is it perhaps the case that the most you can let yourself think possible is that you might—just might—be alive at the same time next year?

Now jump ahead ten years. Let's say you really turn your life around. You fall in with some people who help you kick your drinking problem. They set you up in a job in the mail room of an import-export company. Over the years, you work your way out of the mail room and into the sales department. Eventually, you're promoted to manage a team of salespeople based in China. You find yourself in the business class of a jetliner, flying from Los Angeles to Beijing. You're wiping your hands on a hot towel; flight attendants are offering you sparkling mineral water and extra pillows.

To go from skid row to business class, you have to beat some pretty steep odds. But stories like this aren't unheard of by any means. When you were trying just to make it to the next year, though, do you suppose you were dreaming of hot towels and sparkling water served to you thirty-five thousand feet over the Pacific? Chances are you weren't. Life is often like that: we can see only so far ahead, and to be able to imagine the possibilities once we've reached a certain future point, we sometimes need to just move off in that direction and see what happens next. Life is like traveling on a road with a constant bend in it. You look up ahead, but you can only see as far as the bend allows. Stop and look as hard as you would like. Strain your eyes. You still can only see as far as the bend allows. Travel a bit farther and you can see a bit farther.

We just don't know how things will turn out much of the time. This being the case, the outcomes of our commitments aren't something we have a lot of control over. But moment to moment, we can commit to doing something that will get us a little closer to something that matters to us. And when we fail—and we *will* fail—we'll suddenly find ourselves in a new moment where, once again, we can turn back toward the values we choose. It's in this turning back where you'll find the heart of commitment in ACT.

Appreciating the Plain Fact of Human Sorrow

We live in a culture that doesn't like sorrow much. The signs of it are everywhere. Commercials ask us if we feel anxious or sad and then sell us drugs if the answer is yes. The framers of the new fifth edition of the new *Diagnostic and Statistical Manual of Mental Disorders* are ready to transform bereavement into a disease.

But there's another thing we can do. We can pause. We can take some time. We can appreciate the plain fact of human sorrow.

A few years ago, I was in a conversation about a client who had lost a child in an automobile accident. It brought me to a standstill. Carl Rogers, in his landmark 1961 book *On Becoming a Person*, said "What is most personal is most general." I take that admonition seriously. So, upon hearing of the loss of this child, it seemed right to look deeply into my own experience before responding. I haven't lost a child, but I have lost a brother. I thought about losing Randy and about the meaning of that loss in my own life.

Thoughts of Randy took me to the deep, dark evergreen forests of Western Washington, where my brothers and I grew up. There is a scent in the air in those woods—wet and rich. You can smell life and death in equal abundance. Sometimes a great evergreen would fall. It is sad when you see a big beautiful hemlock crashed to the earth after a hundred years of soaring. Those old trees would lie in the woods for years decomposing, and out of that a neat little row of eight or ten new trees would grow all along that fallen trunk. Slowly, over decades, the trunk would be taken up into the new growth. These fallen trees are called nurse logs.

It turns out that it's very hard for a new tree to find a good spot to germinate and grow on the forest floor. The light is low and the ferns compete for every bit of space and light they can gather. Those fallen trees give the seeds a place above the ferns with a bit more light and moisture and nourishment. If you have an eye for those rows of trees, you can spot them long after the old tree has sunk into the forest floor.

Sometimes in life, new things grow from things that have fallen, not away from them. I find myself wondering, if something new could grow out of the tragedy of a lost child, what might grow there?

And I find myself wondering about the people reading this right now. Do you know about things fallen? About things irrevocably lost? I wonder if you would be willing to stop a moment to acknowledge that loss, to know its face when you see it. If you could grow something new and beautiful from that loss, something that could honor what has fallen, what might that be?

I feel that way about my older brother Randy, who we lost to suicide so many years ago. I have told the story a hundred times in workshops, classes, and coffee shops. I ask people about their own losses. "What would you grow," I ask them, "What would you grow?"

The small trees didn't start growing right away. But the minutes, hours, and days have filled years since that tragic day in 1987—to the brim. And nearly twenty-five years later, I can still see Randy's face, especially his lopsided grin. As I look at all I've nurtured in my life since then, people and projects that stand across the years like seedlings, all in a row, fed by that tragedy, I wonder if he would be proud of me. If he would feel honored by my memory of him.

My own little row of trees can be found in my students, in clients, and in the people around the world who have joined with me in a conversation about meaning and purpose, about the sweet and the sad in life.

I think we owe it to our friends, family, and fellows, to do better than making an illness of the sadness that will surely visit us all one day. Love and loss are poured from the same vessel. There is no way to turn away from what we have lost without turning away from what we have loved.

I invite people—students, clients, you—to come to rest in my little garden where an appreciation of sorrow is not a disease. Let yourself settle in and breathe. Let yourself be saturated. Let a conversation grow up. Let yourself wonder what new things might grow from the rich loam of living.

John Erskine said it beautifully in his 1906 poem "Actæon"

> One drought of Lethe for a world of pain
> An easy bargain; yet I keep the thorn,
> To keep the rose.

Randy? If you're listening? Please know that I remember you, fondly, still, and tend a little garden in your honor.

The Heart of Commitment in ACT

We choose our values and we transform them from words into deeds with commitment: *I will be a good mother to my daughter, I will be kind, I will excel in my profession.* Sure, we make promises about the future—and we fail. We fail often. Sometimes we fail spectacularly. Sometimes it's hard, if not impossible, to imagine a value of any significance that anyone could succeed in furthering all the time. The most loving parent is occasionally self-absorbed and unavailable to his child. The most dedicated professor sometimes blows off her students. Saint Augustine pleaded with God to make him chaste and constant—just not yet. Achievement is wonderful, but perseverance is at the heart of commitment.

◄ THE WELL-STOCKED PANTRY

This exercise is kind of a warm-up to commitment. Start by imagining a pantry, like you might have in your kitchen (or remember from TV shows about life on the prairie). Imagine the shelves empty for the moment. Now, think about some value you hold. Give yourself a few minutes to roll the value around in your head while you consider the following question: If you were going to stock your pantry with acts, both big and small, that would serve this value, what would they be? Put each of these acts into a mason jar or brown paper bag and place them one by one onto the shelves.

Value being a great partner? Maybe your first jar contains a greeting at the front door after your love comes home from a hard day. The second might be listening calmly next time the two of you have a quarrel. On another shelf, maybe there's a little box that contains a time when you will cheerfully agree to the movie or the restaurant of your partner's choice. Just let your pantry fill up with acts you can do. If you fill up one pantry, consider another value and stock up with acts that support it as well.

Let the acts be big and small, but be extra sure to have many very small acts. Acts do not need to be big to be meaningful. Kelly tells a story at workshops about being sick when he was little. When he was sick, his mom would come in and tuck him into bed and lay a gentle hand against his brow to check for fever. Maybe you had a mom like that. Or maybe you wish you had. That small act that took perhaps a minute is remembered fondly by Kelly fifty years after the fact. Some very small acts of kindness can really stretch out over time.

◄

Seen from an ACT perspective, then, there's much more to commitment than just making promises about what will happen tomorrow or the next day. In contrast to the everyday, fixed-and-future sense of commitment, committed action from an ACT perspective involves an ongoing, in-the-moment process of choosing and rechoosing the directions in which we'll move. This nuanced commitment is a dynamic process rather than a static fact, and it has the potential to show up for us in each unfolding moment. More than being a measuring stick for our successes and failures, this kind of commitment is a skill we can refine that will help us reach our goal of finding the freedom to live a rich and meaningful life.

Commitment—Right Now

Commitment is another area where there's an affinity and intimacy between process areas. If commitment seems to recall what we said about present-moment contact, you're getting a good feel for this stuff. The breathing meditation game we described a while back is a very apt metaphor for the kind of commitment we're talking about. If you consider your experiences following your breath, you can observe what commitment from this perspective looks like in flight.

Commitment in ACT links up to a really important type of treatment for depression. The treatment is called *behavioral activation*. Often people think that they need to change how they think in order to do better in life. It turns out that there is very, very good evidence that getting people active produces outcomes as good as antidepressant medications for depression (Dimidjian, et al, 2006). In fact, some forms of behavioral activation contain values elements similar to ACT (Lejuez, et al, in press). We are not made for inactivity. It makes us sick. Living in our heads makes us sick. Getting active is good medicine. Use these commitment processes to gently ease yourself back into the stream of life. Move your body. Engage socially. Eat a healthful meal mindfully, perhaps with good company. Visit a sick friend. Go read to an old person at a nursing home. Walk the dog. Take a yoga class. Engage in even the tiniest acts and watch what happens over time. And the key here really is *over time*. The impact of these things will not likely be immediate. In fact, if you obsessively check to see "if they are working"—meaning *do I feel better?*—you will likely inhibit your development. These acts are not aimed at "feeling better." They are aimed at "living better." Thoughts and feelings will come and go, but a series of small, committed acts, over time, will take you to new places.

The best metaphor for commitment in ACT is a breathing meditation. In the meditation, we bring our awareness to the rise and fall of breath. Even the most dedicated meditator, over time, will find herself making grocery lists in her head, thinking about what is for dinner, the next job, and on and on. In those moments, perhaps we notice that we have strayed from breath.

When we find that is so, we kindly acknowledge straying and gently return to the breath. How many times? We return one more time than we go away. ACT is like a meditation, except the focus is not the breath—it is valued living. No matter how dedicated, we will find ourselves off our values, perhaps in small ways, perhaps in large. When we do, we pause and notice that disconnection from our value and make that gentle return. How many times? *One more time than we turn away.* The heart of commitment is found in that persistent return to a valued pattern of living. Commitment lives and breathes in that moment of return.

AA AND THE GIFT OF COMMITMENT

AA is all about active recovery. This sensibility can be found in the AA basic text. Chapter 6 of *Alcoholics Anonymous* is called "Into Action." In the twelfth step, the larger purpose of all the steps is illuminated in the phrase "we…practice these principles in all our affairs" (AA, 59). In a discussion of the twelfth step in *Twelve Steps and Twelve Traditions*, you'll find "right action is the key to good living" (12 & 12, 125).

One way to think about commitment is to think of it as applied acceptance. One of the things people struggle with a lot when they set out to change their lives is acceptance. And the problem is often with where they go looking for acceptance. Don't put too much effort into seeking acceptance as something you think about. In other words, don't sit around waiting for your mind to agree that something is acceptable. Your mind is not likely to call something acceptable that it has previously cast into the category of "bad" things. Looking for that kind of acceptance is a little like looking for sunny days in Seattle. They happen. When they do happen, they are truly lovely and to be enjoyed. However, you don't want to plan your life around them. You're very unlikely to find acceptance in your head. Even when you do, you can't count on it to show up on the day and in the moment you need it. So, if acceptance is not the thought or feeling of acceptance, what is it?

The kind of acceptance that makes a difference, that changes lives, that invigorates, and that is always available is *lived acceptance*. This kind of acceptance is in your life, not in your head. Even on the rare days when your mind delivers the thought, "Hey, this acceptance stuff is not so bad," little will come of it if it's not backed up by lived values. The good news is that acceptance as lived-values is something that is always available to you. In the ACT model, commitment involves a gentle return to lived values. This is acceptance that walks and talks. It does the next right thing, it takes the next inventory, it makes the next amend, it serves coffee at a meeting, it straightens the chairs afterward, it walks up to a new person at the meeting and says "You're not alone. Together we can do what we couldn't do alone."

People often think about commitment in terms of the future. In ACT, commitment is not about the future. In AA, commitment is not about the future. Even when it comes to drinking, promises about a future of not drinking have little place in AA. Sobriety is a "one day at a time" activity—sometimes one minute or one second at a time.

Commitment to live well, which includes sobriety and a lot more, involves allowing yourself to persistently live in the question that life asks: "In this very moment, am I engaged in right action? What would it look like to pause for a moment, become aware of myself and my actions, and then to make any course correction that puts me in better alignment with what truly matters to me?"

In terms of the steps, the ninth step represents major engagement in commitment processes. Sometimes people think about the amends described in the ninth step as apologies. I don't recommend this approach. An apology may be part of the ninth step, but it's seldom the most important part and may in fact be insulting to the person receiving the apology.

Consider that the root of the word "amend" is the same as "amendment." It means some sort of change that corrects something amiss. For some, life has already consisted of a nearly endless stream of apologies. If this is so, then another apology, no matter how sincerely intended, may not represent any change at all, let alone a change for the better. If you've done your values work in the last chapter and have worked through the fourth through eighth steps, you've likely found that you have been deeply engaged in patterns of living that are at cross purposes with your own most deeply held values. Very often these areas involve your relations with others. Sometimes these breaches of trust take many years to heal.

The world often exhorts people to think big. In fact, we often exhort people to think big and to dream big. However, especially in this area of commitment I want you to remember to *think small*. I advise it for a number of reasons. One reason is that some days, the only thing you will find yourself prepared to do will be a very small act. Go back and take a look at the invitation at the front of the book. Read it carefully. Find this passage in it:

It was a starting point. From there, people began to teach me about acceptance and about holding my story in the world a little more gently, about letting go of limitations and opening up to possibility. By inches, I made my way up off the floor and out of that bathroom.

The key to this passage is "by inches." Life is a game of inches. When it comes to action, often facing a long history of failures, the world seems too much. Those are times to take your eyes from the horizon and look down squarely at your own feet. And, just for today, let inches be enough. Find what you can do, however small, that is in the right direction. Find one tiny action that is in the right direction. Enormous change comes from such small, persistent acts.

This doesn't mean you shouldn't plan. This doesn't mean you shouldn't raise your eyes to the horizon. You should. The AA program suggests it quite directly.

The only urgent thing is that we make a beginning...If we would gain any real advantage in the use of this Step on problems other than alcohol, we shall need to make a brand new venture into open-mindedness. We shall need to raise our eyes toward perfection, and be ready to walk in that direction. *It will seldom matter how haltingly we walk*" (AA 12 & 12, 68).

So we shall have to settle, respecting most of our problems, for a very gradual progress, punctuated sometimes by very heavy setbacks. Our old time attitude of 'all or nothing' will have to be abandoned (AA World Services, Inc., 1999, 6).

And, of course, from the Big Book itself, heard in nearly every meeting in the reading of the steps from "How It Works":

Many of us exclaimed, "What an order! I can't go through with it." Do not be discouraged. No one among us has been able to maintain anything like perfect adherence to these principles. We are not saints. The point is, that we are willing to grow along spiritual lines. The principles we have set down are guides to progress. We claim spiritual progress rather than spiritual perfection (AA, 1976, 60).

Let your life grow from a thousand small committed acts. Some of them will be big, like writing a check for your child support, every single month on exactly the same day (practicing consistency). But let some also be the small committed act of pouring a cup of coffee, straightening chairs, or welcoming a newcomer to the meeting. Each small act builds upon the last. Over time, these small acts will pile up into a tower from which you'll be able to see farther than you could in the past.

Most people learn to play out of their strength. If you do this, you get to play on your strong days, and on your weak days, you have to stay home or lie. You must hide—either literally or you must hide inside of lies that conceal your weakness. If you can learn to play out of both your strength and your weakness, you'll have learned something most people never learn. And, most importantly, you'll get to play every single day.

What does it mean to play out of our weakness? It means noticing where your running, fighting, and hiding have taken you. It means gradually letting go of running, fighting, and hiding in their grosser and subtler forms. It means a gentle return to the patterns of living that you would want mentioned when you have passed from this earth. It means that you bring yourself fully to the table of life each day.

Epilogue

The Next Day, and
the Day After That

We think books are just the beginning of conversations rather than complete conversations unto themselves. It's quite true that this book is just paper (or pixels) until you, reader, consider it and in some way make it your own. The book needed two of us, our teachers, our editors, and our publisher just to get started; you're the one who actually gets to make it into something that matters, by breathing life into these words with your kind attention and good intentions.

We said someplace in the book that we don't really love linearity, that we don't have a lot of confidence that things ever get smoothly from point A to point B. This is never truer for us than with introductions and conclusions. What do we say to "conclude" the book? How the hell do we know?

Recovery has been on Kelly's mind for more than twenty-five years. ACT has occupied his thoughts for most of those years. Troy and Kelly have worked together for five years, and one of their first face-to-face conversations was about the match between ACT and 12-step. In some ways this book brings that conversation full circle. In others, it's just another installment. Our understanding of this stuff will change as we learn from the ways this book is received, in very real ways remaking it as we go along.

You, reader, came to this book for your own reasons. If you've read this far, we're humbled, and we thank you from the bottom of our hearts for your attention. When we decided to put all this down on paper, the goal of serving you was really all we had in mind. We've both tried to bring stillness, varied perspectives, acceptance, a light touch with stories, values, and turning-back-in-kindness commitment into our lives, and we believe, for us, it's been a good thing. We hope it helps you too, in whatever you decide you want your life to be about.

Recovery takes a lifetime, yet it's measured only in moments. With each of them, our hearts and thoughts will be with you. Take care, and best of luck on the journey.

Afterword

SOME THOUGHTS ON THE 12-STEP APPROACH

This is not an AA book by any means. It's a book about using ACT as a model for recovery. This being the case, it's a fair question to ask why we've devoted a good deal of time and book real estate to the discussion of how ACT can be woven into a 12-step recovery approach. The reason is, simply, that 12-step is far and away the most common recovery resource available to people with substance abuse issues, certainly in the United States and also in much of the rest of the Western world. If you're an American with a substance abuse problem, depending on where you reside, AA may be the only source of support available to you while you recover. If your drinking or drug use has gotten you in trouble with the law, the courts may have mandated that you attend AA meetings or receive some kind of 12-step-inspired but professionally mediated treatment. One way or another, most people who wrestle with substance abuse, by choice or not, get some exposure to the 12-step approach to recovery.

We believe that ACT is compatible with 12-step recovery as we understand it. We believe that you can use this book in conjunction with participation in a 12-step program, and neither your work in the book nor your participation in AA, NA, or whichever group you're a part of will suffer as a result. Nevertheless, we made the decision early on not to mash together the ACT material with anything we might have had to say about 12-step. To do so would have been confusing to you, reader, and it wouldn't be doing due diligence insofar as respecting the independence of these two traditions. (Actually, ACT and 12-step do have some common intellectual ancestors, particularly the pragmatic philosophy of William James, but that conversation is very much beyond the scope of this book.)

The reasoning we've used to come to this conclusion is, of course, selective and follows a line that sets out to understand 12-step in a way that's compatible with ACT. If you ask some folks whether our understanding of the 12-step model is right-headed, many will agree that it is. Others may take a more fundamentalist tack and disdain anything that isn't chapter-and-verse AA. This is how the world works, and we wouldn't have it any other way. We'll note this much: Kelly has been training substance abuse counselors all over the world to use ACT principles for more than twenty years, and the responses he has gotten from 12-step-oriented treatment providers have been nearly universally positive.

The Abstinence Question

In the introduction to this book, we took a strong position about abstinence. It was, though, probably not the position that many in the 12-step world would take. Our firm conviction is that the decision to quit or moderate alcohol or drug use is fundamentally personal. And, as we indicated earlier, we know of no convincing evidence that suggests attempts to control drinking or drug use, as opposed to quitting completely, are necessarily doomed to failure.

We realize that this contradicts the broadly held opinion among most treatment centers and also among many within Alcoholics Anonymous. For example, the AA Big Book states that "We know that no real alcoholic *ever* recovers control" (30). We could quibble about definitions. For example, studies show pretty convincingly that some do indeed recover. We could say, "Well, they weren't *real* alcoholics." But if we take the criteria for alcoholism laid out in the major psychiatric diagnostic systems as defining alcoholism, the assertion is quite simply unsustainable. We much prefer the humbler claims found in the Big Book, which assert that "*we,*" meaning the authors of the book, "admitted *we* were powerless over alcohol"—a personal affirmation made by particular individuals.

Many who believe real alcoholics never regain control believe it's dangerous to hold out hope that control is possible. We disagree and know of no systematic evidence that the mere discussion of this idea harms alcoholics. In this matter, we're in full agreement with the Big Book. It suggests that if you think you can return to non-problem drinking, give it a try:

> If anyone who is showing inability to control his drinking can do the right-about-face and drink like a gentleman, our hats are off to him. Heaven knows, we have tried hard enough and long enough to drink like other people!…We do not like to pronounce any individual as alcoholic, but you can quickly diagnose yourself. Step over to the nearest barroom and try some controlled drinking. Try to drink and stop abruptly. Try more than once. It will not take long for you to decide, if you are honest with yourself about it. It may be worth a bad case of jitters if you get a full knowledge of your condition. (31–32)

We like this sentiment much better. It's more agnostic on the issue of control as a general matter. The writers assert that *they* have been unsuccessful and that you'll ultimately have to decide for yourself. We agree with this assertion.

Our position on this issue will probably make some people in AA mad. It will make a lot of the people who believe strongly in the disease model of alcoholism mad. That's just the way it's going to be. We're not writing this book for people with an investment in the categories and labels associated with addiction. We're writing it for you, for people who suffer because of problems with substance abuse. It's not as if people reading this book have never considered the idea that they might moderate their drinking or drug use. In fact, we would be shocked if anyone reading this book had not already made some attempts to moderate drinking or using drugs.

We believe that you're the only one in a position to decide, ultimately, whether another attempt at control is possible or worth the effort for you. That this is the case seems beyond argument to us. It seems consistent with the scientific evidence. It seems consistent with the Big Book. And it seems consistent with the basic idea that your life is your own, that you get to choose your own way, and that the costs such choices incur are a matter only you can evaluate in terms of your own values.

Connecting with 12-Step

Twelve-step programs have been around since the 1930s, beginning with Alcoholics Anonymous. If you're having problems with substances, you almost certainly have some knowledge of AA. In fact, anyone who watches a lot of movies or television has no doubt seen someone standing up at a podium or from their seat in a circle of chairs and saying something like "Hi, my name is Bob, and I'm an alcoholic."

Some people, certainly plenty of people who go to AA, will tell you that AA is the one and only way to get sober. This is simply not true. The Alcoholics Anonymous basic text does not make that claim. Yet a quick look at the research evidence suggests that the approach used in AA is at least as effective as other common evidence-based approaches.

But I Hate AA!

Without a doubt, not everyone finds 12-step programs appealing. (In fact, during their first long conversation a number years ago, long before we started working on this book, Kelly had to disabuse Troy of some long-held—and, truth be told, completely unfounded—biases against the 12-step tradition. These biases are still common enough, especially when they are based more on stories about AA or NA than experience of them.) Even if you have issues with some aspects of 12-step, you can and should feel free to take from that tradition anything that might be of use to you, including the support of a community of others in recovery.

We've collected a checklist of reasons people hate AA. Some of the reasons are misunderstandings and some are genuine objections, but we think they can be worked with. Let's take a look at them.

I hate AA because:

I don't want to be confronted, accused of being in denial, and called an alcoholic. We feel the same way. Don't put up with it. There are no data showing that confrontation is an effective treatment strategy. Although AA is often thought of as confrontational, it's definitely not—or, at least, it was never intended to be. Many treatment centers that are allegedly AA-oriented are confrontational, but the confrontation has nothing whatsoever to do with AA.

The concept of denial and a client's desire to drink or use moderately rather than quitting entirely are intimately linked in the 12-step-oriented treatment community. According to the Big Book, "The idea that somehow, someday he will control and enjoy his drinking is the great obsession of every abnormal drinker...We learned that we had to fully concede to our innermost selves that we were alcoholics. This is the first step in recovery. The delusion that we are like other people, or presently may be, has to be smashed" (AA, 30). Presumably some treatment providers consider this a basis for the claim that anyone who shows drinking problems and wants to moderate is in denial and ought to be confronted. However, the position the AA literature articulates is much more complex.

Nowhere in the AA literature can you find the words "confronting denial" or any instance in which one member is reported to have confronted another. AA staunchly advocates self-diagnosis as the only useful or meaningful diagnosis. The Big Book suggests that, among those with drinking problems, "Some will moderate or stop altogether, and some will not" (AA, 109). And, in AA's advice on working with others, they suggest telling individuals who are reluctant to quit entirely that they may be able to control their drinking if they are not "too alcoholic" (AA, 1976, 92).

If self-deception is to be smashed, it's not to be done by another member of AA or by a treatment center. Rather, this conclusion will come about because of the drinker's own experience that drinking does not work. The lives of people with substance-abuse issues are often marked by confrontation: by authorities, medical personnel, employers, family members, friends. You may have already experienced quite a bit of this. Has it moved you? Done anything significant to motivate you to change? If confrontation were a constructive approach to helping abusers change, recovery would likely be a lot easier. The culture at large provides no shortage of confrontation.

If anyone within AA confronts you about your problems with drinking or drug use, you might consider reading him or her some of the quotations above and ask to be shown, in the Big Book or the 12 steps and 12 traditions, where AA recommends name calling and confrontation.

And this goes for you, too. Just because everyone at AA starts to speak by saying, "Hi, my name is Bob, and I'm an alcoholic," doesn't mean you have to follow suit. If you find yourself in this situation and you choose not to take up the label "alcoholic," try this: "My name is Bob and I'm grateful to be here." Or, "My name is Bob and I lost a wrestling match with alcohol." Some people might not like it. Let them not like it. Their liking isn't required. You're not at the meeting to make other people happy. You're there to recover.

I hate the idea of having a disease. The idea that alcoholism and addiction is a disease is actually quite controversial. Usually people think this is an AA idea. It's not. In fact, none of the AA basic texts say that alcoholism is a disease. Describing the condition broadly, the Big Book refers to alcoholism as "an illness which only a spiritual experience will conquer" (AA, 44). In 1961, AA founder Bill Wilson described the organization's position:

We have never called alcoholism a disease because, technically speaking, it is not a disease entity. For example, there is no such thing as heart disease. Instead there are many separate heart ailments, or combinations of them. It is something like that with alcoholism. Therefore we did not wish to get in wrong with the medical profession by pronouncing alcoholism a disease entity. Therefore we always called it an illness, or a malady—a far safer term for us to use. (Kurtz 2002, 22)

In fact, until very recently, there was just about no place in any of the AA or NA literature that called these problems "diseases," yet many, many people within AA and NA believe in the disease model. Perhaps this is what they were told in treatment or were told by others in AA who, in their turn, got the concept in treatment. But it's worth noting that, by design, AA is made up completely and solely of its members. The organization has taken some pains to not recognize authorities or experts within its ranks, and professionally mediated treatment programs are explicitly outside the traditional scope of AA. Recognizing addiction as a disease, given our cultural expectations about health and wellness, does reasonably lead to the idea that there must be a doctor or other professional to treat that disease. The tenth tradition of AA holds that "Alcoholics Anonymous has no opinion on outside issues; hence the AA name ought never be drawn into public controversy." Whether or not alcoholism is or isn't a disease is a matter for scientists to sort out. People within 12-step programs generally don't have the means or training to determine this. And just because the idea is popular does not mean that it's correct.

The scientific community is quite divided. We could certainly be proved wrong in this matter. In the end, it doesn't matter all that much. People were getting sober in AA before the widespread adoption of the idea that alcoholism is a disease. And no matter which way the science goes, AA will have exactly the same benefit.

Think of it this way: imagine that some people thought mountain climbing was a disease. They could point to people who continue to climb, even after they lose toes and fingers to frostbite, even after their spouses divorce them because of extended time away climbing. If there were a program that helped people stay off mountains, it would work or not to the extent that it accomplished its stated goals of keep mountaineers at home in the flatlands, whether mountain climbing was a disease or not.

Maybe alcoholism is a disease, and maybe it's not. You don't have to figure this out to recover. And you don't have to figure it out to use AA. If you're going to AA, we don't recommend you argue with people about this. Doing so will be a waste everyone's time. And for the purposes of getting sober, it just doesn't matter. We suggest you focus your attention on things that matter. The bottom line is, if you think you have a problem rather than a disease, you're in good company.

I don't want to be going to meetings forever. Okay, so don't. Don't go to meetings forever. We mentioned at the beginning that you can put this book through its paces without ever setting foot into an AA meeting. We think there may be value in the experience of AA meetings for some people trying to recover, and if you don't know whether they're right for you, the best advice we can think of is to suggest you attend a few and find out. If and when you do, nothing says you have to keep showing up. You may find you want to. Many find fellowship and support at AA that they treasure for a lifetime. Others stop going after some period of time.

Some at AA will tell you that people who quit going to AA get drunk. They will sometimes say, "I go to meetings to see what happens to people who don't go to meetings." These folks often have the experience of watching people stop coming, get drunk, and come back with tales about how not going to meetings caused the trouble. This may seem like good common sense, but it's bad logic. Some people who quit going to meetings get drunk and some don't. The ones who don't have little incentive to come back and report on their successes. They're just out there living their lives. As with everything else we've been talking about, meeting attendance is, we strongly feel, a matter of personal choice. We said in the section on commitment: If you choose to attend meetings for a while, stop, and then start drinking or using again, our hope is to help you find a way to turn back to what worked for you, in kindness to yourself. If you decide to go to a meeting, go to it *for now* and let later take care of itself.

I hate all the God stuff. Without a doubt, there's a lot of God stuff going on at AA. And while there is certainly a segment of people in AA who would chafe at the suggestion, the plain fact is that "God," in the context of AA literature, is a substitute for "your own particular spiritual beliefs."

The tradition of tolerance for various spiritual beliefs in AA is goes back to the organization's earliest days. The first AA member, Bill Wilson, was from New York. While traveling on business, Wilson called on the second AA member, Dr. Bob Smith, in Akron, Ohio. Dr. Bob, as he has since come to be known, had been very involved with an organization called the Oxford Group. Wilson had also been exposed to that group, but shied away from some of its authoritarian spiritual doctrine. In the early years of AA, had it been left entirely to the Akron faction of AA, there would have likely been a far stricter set of spiritual views in AA. But those darned New Yorkers were a more diverse lot and did not much like being told what to believe or what to do.

As result, the Big Book refers again and again to the idea of *God as we understood Him* and to the even more generic concept of a *Higher Power*. In fact, depending on where you are in the country, you may find a lot of people disaffected with organized religion in AA. Depending on where you live, this will vary. If you live in the Bible Belt, you will find a lot of Baptists. If you live in certain parts of Boston, you are likely to find a lot of Catholics. If you live in western Massachusetts, you will likely run into a lot of Buddhists. It's possible to find people with all manner of beliefs who have found AA useful, including people who believed in traditional religions, but also individuals who regarded nature, love, or human fellowship as a higher power. There are even committed atheists who are committed members of AA.

As described above, this relative openness is by design. Here is what Bill Wilson had to say on the topic in his book *Alcoholics Anonymous Comes of Age*:

Who first suggested the actual compromise words I don't know, but they are words well-known throughout the length and breadth of AA today: In Step Two we decided to describe God as a "Power greater than ourselves." In Steps Three and Eleven we inserted the words "God as we understood him." From Step Seven we deleted the expression "on our knees." And, as a lead-in sentence to all the steps we wrote the words: "Here are the steps we took which are suggested as a Program of Recovery." AA's Twelve Steps were to be suggestions only.

Such were the final concessions to those of little or no faith; this was the great contribution of our atheists and agnostics. They had widened our gateway so that all who suffer might pass through, regardless of their belief or lack of belief. (Alcoholics Anonymous 1957, 167)

If you go to AA and anyone tries to bully you about spiritual matters, show them this quotation from one of their own books and calmly ask them to show you where in any of the AA texts it says that members should bully other members about their spiritual beliefs. They will likely shut up. Folks in AA generally have respect for the AA texts. Wilson is clearly acknowledging the contributions of people who struggle with this aspect of the program, just like you. They made a contribution to AA, and so can you. If you go online and search AA and atheism, you'll get many, many hits. Some will go on a tirade about AA being a religious cult. Some will say participation in AA is impossible if you're an atheist. But some will say things like, "I've been sober in AA for twenty years and am as much an atheist as I was the day I walked in the door." Clearly, it's possible. More challenging? Maybe. But if you're an atheist reading these sentences, that challenge is something you already know about.

What about Equal Rights for Women, Sensitivity to Minorities, Gay Rights!?

Okay, you definitely have us on this one. No two ways about it: the AA Big Book was written by white men and about white men. The newer editions have tended to include more stories of women, but the main text does not show the slightest sensitivity to gender issues. For example, there is a chapter called "To Wives" but not a chapter called "To Husbands" or "To Partners." And, of course, God is definitely a guy. Kelly once interviewed a woman in Spokane, WA, who got sober in Chicago in the 1950s. She reported that she had to practically physically fight her way into the AA meetings. They insisted that she should go with the wives. AA was a men's club. This should not be a shock to us. The fight for equality for all is a long and hard road. People are very, very reluctant to tinker with the first 164 pages of the AA Big Book. We expect it will come eventually. AA is getting bigger and more diverse by the year. For now, we recommend you read the Big Book as a historical document. It carries the language of the time in which it was written. We hope that if you can look past these flaws, you will find that many people from many backgrounds have found sobriety in 12-step programs. Who knows, twenty years down the road, perhaps history will look back and see that this year was the year that "differences" reached critical mass in AA that ultimately changed some of that language.

12-Step and Workability

AA has a deeply practical side. "Take what you can use and leave the rest" is a common AA adage. The title of chapter 5 of the Big Book is "How It Works." This chapter lays out the AA approach to recovery as a series of twelve steps, but before that section commences, the authors of that book state: "Here are the steps we took, which are suggested as a program of recovery" (AA, 59). We prefer to think that the word "suggested" in this context was carefully chosen. The authors of the AA text very often default to a very local and humble assessment of the facts as they see them. The texts are littered with phrases like "we have found" and "alcoholics of our type." There are many statements such as this one: "Our book is meant to be suggestive only. We realize we know only a little" (AA, 164). These simple assertions, we believe, are the best of what AA has to offer. If you go to AA and hear dogmatism and absolutes, we can only conclude that you're hearing opinions that evolved independently of the base AA literature.

Have we been selective in our approach to the AA texts? You bet! Are we providing *the* correct way of understanding AA? Not by any means! We're providing just one way of understanding AA that may be useful to you. And we would recommend that you be selective too. If you find things in AA that you object to, let them be and come back to them later. Some of these you may see in a different light with more time spent in the act of recovery. In reconsidering some, you may find yourself surprised that you were so put off about them early on. And some may continue not to sit well with you. All possible options are fine. We recommend you not let a single objection, or even a set of objections, dissuade you from exploring what benefits you might find in AA.

The Third Tradition of AA

AA and other 12-step programs probably contain the same percentage of jerks as can be found in the culture as a whole. You can find bullies and know-it-alls at the office, at the supermarket, and yes, at an AA meeting. Fortunately, there's a way that you can inoculate yourself against these views. AA's recovery process is famously divided into the 12 steps. Lesser known, perhaps, are AA's 12 traditions. These are elaborated most clearly in the publication *Twelve Steps and Twelve Traditions*. Especially important for our purposes is the third tradition: "The only requirement for AA membership is a desire to stop drinking" (139). The door to AA is left wide open by the inclusion of this tradition. In the early days of AA, described in *Twelve Steps and Twelve Traditions* and elsewhere, there were many requirements for membership. Ultimately they were all dropped because the membership wanted to keep the doors open to all who sought help. In its earliest versions there was language suggesting the need for an "honest" desire to stop drinking. Even that was seen as a potential bar to some who might seek help. Any desire at all is enough, and you are, by the rules of AA, a member when you say you are. There's only one person who can revoke your membership and that is you.

This does not mean that, if you stand up at an AA meeting and declare that you're a devout atheist, everyone will applaud and tell you that you're welcome. Many will not. But try that same thing at a restaurant or at a local park. You'll no doubt find people happy to point out the error in your thinking in the strongest terms. But the people who have opinions that are different than yours have absolutely no power to revoke your membership. Your place in the meeting and the community is assured by the third tradition. Stick with AA for a while and see what the results are. Or, try something different. We're sure that if what you try doesn't work, you'll be able to tell, and your own sense of what works and what doesn't will matter more than anyone else's opinion. Here is what they ask in the 12 & 12: "Why did we dare say…that we would neither punish nor deprive any A.A. of membership, that we must never compel anyone to pay anything, believe anything, or conform to anything?" They feared that telling people what to do might exclude someone from help. Their answer to that question: "Who dared to be judge, jury, and executioner of his own brother?" (141). Whatever path, you chose it. Our sincerest wish is that this book helps carry you on your way.

FURTHER STUDY

Some people like to read. Some don't. This list is for you if you're in the first camp.

Something that we never got around to mentioning in the book is that knowing doesn't mean all that much. It's always been the case (ever met a drunk who didn't *know* he should quit drinking?), and now that virtually every one of us carries around instant *access to each and every single thing known to mankind* in our pockets (as long as we pay the bills on our smartphones), knowing stuff probably matters even less. The magic is in the doing, not the knowing. Instead of things you should read, think of the resources below as roads you might consider traveling. Happy trails.

Beautiful Writers

What do these writers and their work have to do with recovery? Nothing, and everything. Start a conversation with any one of these folks, and you can change your life forever. There's no need for us to recommend specific titles here; the names are enough. Search by name on the Internet, at your local library, or at a bookstore.

- Albert Camus

- Carolyn Elkins

- Naiomi Shihab Nye

- Robert Frost

- Rudyard Kipling

- Sebastian Moore

- T. S. Eliot

- Viktor Frankl

Books on ACT

If you like the whole ACT thing, there's plenty for you to read. We have a couple of earlier books that cover some of the same ground this one does, only with different applications. *Things Might Go Terribly, Horribly Wrong* (New Harbinger 2010) is a book written for people struggling with anxiety, and *Mindfulness for Two* (New Harbinger 2008) is a book written for clinicians (although anyone can get the gist of it) about what it means to be genuinely present with a client (or, really, any other human being). With our dear friend and colleague Emily Sandoz, we also wrote a couple of books that apply this work to eating disorders: *Acceptance and Commitment Therapy for Eating Disorders* (New Harbinger 2010) and *The Mindfulness and Acceptance and Workbook for Bulimia* (New Harbinger 2011). These are obviously not for everyone, but they make use of many of the same concepts as this book—so someone in your life might be interested.

Another take on ACT (one that reads very differently from our books) is Steven Hayes and Spencer Smith's very popular book *Get Out of Your Mind and Into Your Life* (New Harbinger 2006). This book isn't written for any particular problem or challenge; it's just a general introduction to ACT. If depression is something you struggle with, *The Mindfulness and Acceptance Workbook for Depression* (New Harbinger 2008), by Kirk Strosahl and Patricia Robinson, is a great choice (and it comes with some really excellent audio exercises). The original book

Acceptance and Commitment Therapy (Guilford Press, first edition 1999, second edition due out in October of 2011), by Steven Hayes, Kirk Strosahl, and yours truly, Kelly Wilson, is a challenging book written for scholars and clinicians, but if you really get interested in this work, you might give it a read.

Books on AA

Throughout this book, we've referred to *Alcoholics Anonymous*, known as the Big Book (Alcoholics Anonymous World Services, Inc. 2002), and *The Twelve Steps and Twelve Traditions*, known as 12 & 12 (A. A. Grapevine, Inc, and Alcoholics Anonymous World Services, Inc. 2002). You can buy these books in paper editions, or you can access the complete text of either for free online at www.aa.org/bigbookonline and www.aa.org/1212, respectively.

For some amazing insights into AA work and a unique take on AA's history, we recommend the books of Ernie Kurtz: *Not God* (Hazelden 1991), *The Spirituality of Imperfection* (Bantam 1993), and *Shame and Guilt* (iUniverse 2007).

Online Groups and Resources

The Association of Contextual Behavior Science is a professional organization that loosely organizes folks who are part of the ACT community. Its website, contextualpsychology.org, has quite a few useful resources, including a directory of ACT therapists you can browse. Some of the content on the site is available to members only, but membership is open to interested nonprofessionals, and the dues are values-based: you only need to pay what you think membership is worth to you (as long as it's at least $1).

There are numerous online resources for AA, the most significant of which is www.aa.org.

There is an online group called ACT for the Public. It is a discussion group of people using ACT for all sorts of different difficulties from substance abuse to anxiety to depression. You can join it by going to http://health.groups.yahoo.com/group/ACT_for_the_Public/

You will find fellow travelers there, including Kelly, who is a semi-frequent contributor to the discussion.

REFERENCES

A.A. Grapevine, Inc, and Alcoholics Anonymous World Services, Inc. 1981. *Twelve Steps and Twelve Traditions* (12 & 12). New York: Alcoholics Anonymous World Services, Inc.

AA World Services, Inc. 1998. *Living Sober.* New York: AA World Services, Inc.

———. 1999. *As Bill Sees It: The A. A. Way of Life (Selected Writings of A.A.'s Co-Founder).* New York: AA World Services, Inc.

Abramowitz, J. S., D. F. Tolin, and G. P. Street. 2001. Paradoxical effects of thought suppression: A meta-analysis of controlled studies. *Clinical Psychology Review* 21(5), 683-703.

Alcoholics Anonymous. 1957. *Alcoholics Anonymous Comes of Age.* New York: Alcoholics Anonymous World Services.

Alcoholics Anonymous World Services, Inc. 2008. *Alcoholics Anonymous* (The Big Book). New York: Alcoholics Anonymous World Services, Inc.

Baumeister, R. F., J. D. Campbell, J. I. Krueger, and K. D. Vohs. 2005. Exploding the self-esteem myth. *Scientific American Mind,* January, 50–57.

Cohen, G. L., J. Garcia, N. Apfel, and A. Master. 2006. Reducing the racial achievement gap: A social-psychological intervention. *Science 313*, 1307-131

Cresswell, J. D., W. T. Welch, S. E. Taylor, D. K. Sherman, T. L. Gruenewald, and T. Mann. 2005. Affirmation of personal values buffers neuroendocrine and psychological stress responses. *Psychological Science* 16: 11.

Dickson, J. *Humilitas: A Lost Key to Life, Love, and Leadership.* 2011. Grand Rapids, MI: Zondervan.

Diimidjian, S., S. D. Hollon, K. S. Dobson, K. B. Schmaling, R. J. Kohlenberg, et al. 2006. Randomized trial of behavioral activation, cognitive therapy, and antidepressant medication in the acute treatment of adults with major depression. *Journal of Consulting and Clinical Psychology* Aug;74(4):658–70.

Frankl, V. E. 1984. *Man's Search for Meaning.* New York: Touchstone.

Gifford, E. V., J. B. Ritsher, J. D. McKellar, and R. H. Moos. 2006. Acceptance and relationship context: A model of substance use disorder treatment outcome. *Addiction* 101(8), 1167–1177.

Hayes, S. C., F. W. Bond, A. Masuda, and J. Lillis. 2006. Acceptance and commitment therapy: Model, processes, and outcomes. *Behaviour Research and Therapy* 44(1), 1–25.

Kabat-Zinn, J. 2006. *Coming to Our Senses.* New York: Hyperion.

Kurtz, E. 1991. *Not God.* Center City, MN: Hazelden.

Kurtz, E. 2002. Alcoholics Anonymous and the disease concept of alcoholism. *Alcoholism Treatment Quarterly* 2002, 20(3/4), 31.

Lejuez, C. W., D. R. Hopko, R. Acierno, S. B. Daughters, and S. L. Pagoto. In press. Ten year revision of the brief behavioral activation treatment for depression (BATD): Revised treatment manual (BATD-R). *Behavior Modification.*

Luoma, J. B., B. S. Kohlenberg, S. C. Hayes, and L. Fletcher. In press. Slow and steady wins the race: A randomized clinical trial of acceptance and commitment therapy targeting shame in substance use disorders. *Journal of Consulting and Clinical Psychology.*

Maisto, S. A., P. R. Clifford, R. L. Stout, and C. M. Davis. 2006. Drinking in the year after treatment as a predictor of three-year drinking outcomes. *Journal of Studies on Alcohol 67*, 823–832.

Pennebaker, J. W., and S. K. Beall. 1986. Confronting a traumatic event: Toward an understanding of inhibition and disease. *Journal of Abnormal Psychology* 95(3), 274–281.

Purdon, C. 1999. Thought suppression and psychopathology. *Behaviour Research and Therapy* 37(11), 1029–1054.

Roemer, L., and T. D. Borkovec. 1994. Effects of suppressing thoughts about emotional material. *Journal of Abnormal Psychology* 103(3), 467–474.

Spera, S., E. Buhrfeind, and J. W. Pennebaker. 1994. Expressive writing and coping with job loss. *Academy of Management Journal* 37(3), 722–733.

Vaillant, G.E. 1995. *The Natural History of Alcoholism Revisited*. Cambridge, MA: Harvard University Press.

Wood, J. V., W. Q. Perunovic, and J. W. Lee. 2009. "Positive Self-Statements: Power for some, peril for others." *Psychological Science*, 20 (7) 860–866.

Wegner, D. M, D. J. Schneider, S. R. Carter III, and T. L. White.1987. Paradoxical effects of thought suppression. *Journal of Personality and Social Psychology* 1987, 53, 636–647

Kelly G. Wilson, PhD, is associate professor of psychology at the University of Mississippi. He is coauthor of *Acceptance and Commitment Therapy, Mindfulness for Two,* and *Things Might Go Terribly, Horribly Wrong.* He is a trainer and speaker in the areas of acceptance and commitment therapy and behavior analysis and lives and works in Oxford, MS. www.onelifellc. com.

Troy DuFrene is a writer who specializes in psychology and has coauthored several books, including *Coping with OCD; Mindfulness for Two; Things Might Go Terribly, Horribly Wrong; Acceptance and Commitment Therapy for Eating Disorders;* and *The Mindfulness and Acceptance Workbook for Bulimia.* He lives in the San Francisco Bay Area. www.troydufrene.com

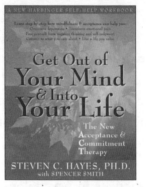

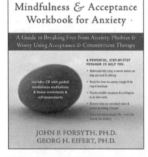